HOW TO

SEND SMOKE SIGNALS, PLUCK A CHICKEN & BUILD AN IGLOO

How to Send Smoke Signals, Pluck a Chicken & Build an Igloo is the North American edition of *How to Send Smoke Signals and Other Vital Life Skills* (2014), originally published by Baker & Taylor UK Ltd. This version published in 2019 by Fox Chapel Publishing Company, Inc., 903 Square Street, Mount Joy, PA 17552. No part of this publication may be reproduced, stored in a retrieval system or transmitted, in any form or by any means, electronic, mechanical, photocopying, recording or otherwise, without the prior written permission of the copyright holders.

Project Team (UK Edition)
Text by Michael Powell
Book layout by Bag of Badgers Ltd

Project Team (North America Edition)
Vice President–Content: Christopher Reggio
Editor: Laura Taylor
Designer: David Fisk

ISBN 978-1-4971-0049-7

Library of Congress Control Number: 2019945996.

To learn more about the other great books from Fox Chapel Publishing, or to find a retailer near you, call toll-free 800-457-9112 or visit us at *www.FoxChapelPublishing.com*.

We are always looking for talented authors. To submit an idea, please send a brief inquiry to acquisitions@foxchapelpublishing.com.

Printed in Malaysia
First printing

HOW TO

SEND SMOKE SIGNALS, PLUCK A CHICKEN, & BUILD AN IGLOO

PLUS **75** ADDITIONAL SKILLS YOU NEVER KNEW YOU NEEDED

— **MICHAEL POWELL** —

FOX CHAPEL
PUBLISHING

CONTENTS

A cornucopia of life skills to learn!

Introduction

The vast majority of people enjoy the natural world, but many of us are unaware just what an incredible natural resource awaits beyond our front doors, or we are intimidated by our lack of knowledge of the wild places. However, everyone is capable of learning traditional skills to tame the wilderness and to deepen their understanding and enjoyment of nature. We would all benefit from a crash course in outdoor living.

Most of us haven't got the first clue about the easiest al fresco tasks, let alone how to track animals or build a dry stone wall. But nothing is more important than getting back to basics! Nothing! That's why you'll love this book. It's an indispensable collection of practical, straightforward advice—everything you need to start facing the challenges of the great outdoors.

It is a pocket compendium of more than seventy wilderness skills to boost your open-air basics, from plucking a chicken and collecting maple syrup to shoeing a horse and opening a coconut with a stone. Keep it handy so that you can refer to it whenever you need to start a fire in the rain, read a compass, forage for food, sharpen a knife, or survive a bear attack. It's reassuring to discover that many seemingly complicated tasks are quite simple when broken down into their basic, essential steps.

Some of the skills in this book require a bit of practice, but in the words of Eighties pop band The Korgis, "everybody's got to learn sometime" and everybody's got to start somewhere too. Even an expert has to begin with the nuts and bolts. Despite this, the hope is that you could actually study topics like "make a dugout canoe" or "pan for gold" and disappear for a few weeks to turn a fallen tree into an open boat or find your fortune in a local stream.

Reading this book won't make you a master of primitive technology overnight but it will certainly put you ahead of the game, point you in the right direction, and show that some of the skills you considered beyond your reach are extremely accessible.

STOP A RUNAWAY HORSE

When a horse gets spooked and starts to run away with you on its back, acting quickly and calmly is the only way to avoid taking a dirt bath and breaking bones.

If you tense up, shout, and scream for help or try to brutalize the horse into submission by yanking indiscriminately on the reins, you will simply make the horse more frightened, putting you in even greater danger.

Don't be tempted to pull the Spaghetti Western trick of ripping your shirt off and using it to blindfold the horse or pulling hard on one rein to make him gallop in a tight circle. Westerns have taught us a lot of silly myths about horses, not least that riding them is easy! Both of these methods are the equivalent of turning off your headlights and punching yourself in the jaw while driving the wrong way on a highway. If the horse can't see, it may slam on the brakes but it may also run into a tree before it comes to a halt. Meanwhile, if you are exerting several hundred pounds of painful rein pressure on its jaw, you become part of the problem.

STOPPING A HORSE MEANS CONTROLLING ITS MIND SO YOU CAN REGAIN CONTROL OF ITS BODY:

1. Focus first on riding the horse rather than stopping him. Allow the horse to see where he is going while you concentrate on keeping your balance.

2. Stay calm, loose, and relaxed. Stiffening your muscles will only give you a rougher ride, making it harder for you to keep your balance. Focus instead on keeping your body relaxed and upright, allowing your body to absorb the horse's galloping rhythm.

3. Keep your legs in soft contact with the horse as you become attuned to his surges and begin squeezing a little with your legs each time, then relaxing to allow the stride. This brings you more in synch with the horse and helps him to calm down and trust your judgment. Think about using your legs to reassure by framing rather than dominate him into submission (good luck with that).

4. Gradually take back control and begin to shape the horse's strides so that eventually you can stop the horse by using the conventional commands that he has already learned. He hasn't forgotten those commands, but he won't pay attention to them unless you help him to calm down first.

PITCH A TENT
without tent poles

If you roll up at your campsite miles from anywhere and then suddenly discover that you've left the tent poles at home, here's a neat way to get Around the problem.

1. Find an overhanging tree, or a tree with a horizontal branch that is a couple of feet higher than the top of your tent.

2. Tie a rope around the tree trunk/branch and let the loose end hang downwards. This is the center point of the tent roof, so lay out your tent underneath and stake the corners of the tent to the ground.

3. Measure and cut two lengths of rope. Feed one through the front right corner to the back right corner; feed the other one through the front left corner to the back left corner, so you end up with two parallel loops.

4. Attach the two loops to the loose end of cord hanging down from the tree, using a tab (you should have one on each guy rope). Tighten vertically until the tent is taut.

5. Use your remaining guy ropes to pull the tent fabric outward to shape and secure the tent.

First find a tree that is suitable for climbing: it should provide sufficient challenge to push you out of your comfort zone, but not so you face serious danger. Only you can be the judge of this. Dry conditions are the best for climbing.

CLIMB A TREE

1. Don't look down. Look up and focus on finding a climbing route using safe branches.

2. Always keep at least three points of contact with the tree, so that if a hand or foot slips, you can support your weight with the other two.

3. Lean up against the trunk to gain maximum stability and place your feet where the branch meets the trunk, where it is thickest and strongest. The further away from the trunk you place your feet, the greater the leverage on the branch and the greater the risk of it breaking.

4. The branches get thinner the higher you climb. Usually, a branch will be strong enough to support your weight if it is as thick as your upper arm. Beware of dead branches.

5. Your legs are much stronger than your arms, so use your legs to do most of the climbing work.

6. When descending, support all your weight with one leg and two hands as you locate a lower branch with your other leg. Test the branch by releasing your weight onto it gradually.

CATCH A FISH
in a trap

One of the least labor-intensive ways to catch fish in the wild is to build a river bank corral made from sticks or stones. Since the Mesolithic era, hunter-gatherers have built structures in streams and rivers or at the edge of tidal lagoons to trap fish. This method has the advantage that you don't have to sit around with a rod or spear waiting for your meal to arrive. You can go away and enjoy a leisurely nap before returning to claim your prize.

1. Collect a pile of about sixty sticks, ¾-1½ in (2-4 cm) thick and about 20 in (50 cm) long, which you will use to construct a small, rectangular enclosure at the water's edge. If there are no sticks, use stones.

2. First make the two long sides of your enclosure with one end facing upstream by driving two parallel lines of sticks/stones into the river bed to form a corridor about 20 in (50 cm) wide and jutting out about 30 in (75 cm) into the water, or until you reach a depth of water that a fish can swim in.

3. Seal off the far end of the enclosure by making a funnel of sticks/rocks pointing into the shore with a 4 in (10 cm) gap—wide enough to allow a fish to swim through.

4. Skewer some bait on a stick and then drive the stick into the river bed so that the bait is exposed underwater inside the enclosure about 8 in (20 cm) from the funnel entrance.

5. Any fish entering the funnel to take the bait will then either swim in a circle or wedge itself nose first into the space on either side of the entrance, where it will stay alive and fresh, ready for you to eat.

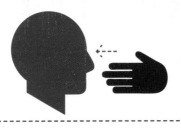

LEARN

FINGER WHISTLING

There are certain situations where only a finger whistle will rise to the occasion—enthusiastically supporting your team in a rambunctious sport or attracting the attention of a friend above the din of a buoyant crowd spring easily to mind. Some people are natural whistlers who seem to effortlessly summon ear-piercing calls to action, but the rest of us mere mortals need a little instruction.

The basic principle is to use your fingers to create a "whistle" shape through which you blow to magnify the sound.

The combination of fingers depends on the size of your mouth and fingers. The one-handed approach uses the thumb and any one of your other fingers (index and middle are the most popular). The two-hander usually uses the index and middle fingers of both hands.

1. Wet and tuck back your top and bottom lips to cover your teeth (as if you were pretending to be a toothless old crone).

2. Position each finger halfway between the corner of your mouth and the center of your lips and insert up to the first knuckle.

3. Touch the fingertips together and angle them in toward the center of your tongue to create a horizontal "A" shape.

4. Draw back your tongue so that the tip is almost touching the floor of your mouth a little way behind your lower teeth. (This is important as it means your tongue is broadened to cover more of your lower back teeth.) Your fingers keep your tongue pushed back, and they also keep your lips tucked back over your teeth.

5. Take a deep breath and blow, forcing the air over your fingers and lower lip.

Fortunately, anyone can learn to whistle but great power requires the utmost discretion. For example, your new skill will impress nobody in the Royal Box at Wimbledon nor will it attract the attention of a waiter in an exclusive restaurant.

MAKE NATURAL FIBER CORD

There are numerous plants whose leaves and/or stems are suitable for making strong natural cordage, from dogbane and milkweed to stinging nettles and Douglas Iris.

You can also use the fibrous inner bark from some trees (e.g., the dead branches of cedar or white basswood). Here is a simple method using stinging nettles.

Nettles have been used for cordage for thousands of years as they have very long fibers, but you do need to gather a lot of them. The best nettles for cordage are the purple-stemmed red nettles that have stronger fibers than the green-stemmed variety.

1. First cut about forty nettles, with stems about 3 ft (90 cm) long.

2. Strip the leaves from the stems. You can use your bare hands, by gripping each leaf firmly where it meets the stem and then snapping it off. But it is quicker to use gloves, because this allows you to run your index finger and thumb along the stem and strip the leaves in just a few seconds.

3. Flatten the stripped stem by squashing it between your finger and thumb, then split open to reveal the green pith.

4. Holding the stem in the middle, pith side up, snap the stem so the pith breaks. Then trap the intact purple outer stem between index finger and thumb and pull the purple stem down so that it separates from the pith. Repeat with the other half, until you are left with two purple fibers.

5. You can use them immediately but your cord will be much stronger if you dry the fibers before rolling into cordage.

6. To make the cord, twist a couple of fibers together and roll them on your thigh with your palm until they are even and round.

7. Bend this double fiber in two and hold the middle with your left hand.

8. Roll the two parallel strands forward on your thigh at the same time, then at the end of the roll trap them with your palm and release your left hand and you'll see the twist transfer into the loop that you have just released.

9. Give it a couple of counterclockwise twists with your left hand to help it tighten and you will have a couple of inches of cord.

10. Repeat steps 8 and 9 with the next few inches of fiber to gain another couple of inches of cord.

11. When you are close to running out of fiber on the right hand side, simply add another fiber as you perform the rolling, so that your cord continues to grow without interruption.

AGE A TREE WITHOUT CUTTING IT DOWN

Everyone knows the easy way to age a tree—cut it down and count the growth rings. The trouble is there's an obvious flaw in this method: it kills the tree.

Fortunately there are several other ways to age a tree without resorting to this terminal solution. Here are four of them.

CORE EXTRACTION

You can use a specialized drilling tool to count tree rings without damaging the tree. An increment borer is a special drill consisting of a handle, a drilling bit, and a small core extractor that fits into the auger bit. Drill into the tree at chest height using a borer the length of which is at least 75 percent of the tree's diameter. Put your body weight into the first few turns to get it going, making sure to keep the drill horizontal.

Keep turning the handle until the end of the well-lubricated drill reaches just a little farther than half way (i.e., just past the pith—the tree center).

While the tool is still in the tree, carefully introduce the core extractor through the back of the drill. Make sure the open side of the extractor is facing downward. Then make one-half turn of the drill in the reverse direction and then slowly withdraw the core extractor.

Now count the rings. Most trees produce two rings each year: one light spring ring and a darker summer ring. You can count either to determine the age of the tree. Add on a few years to allow for the early growth that won't show up in your sample.

COUNT THE WHORLS

Each year a new whorl is created when a bud bursts through the tip of the tree to form a new branch. In some species counting tree whorls (spiral scars on the trunk) can give a rough estimate of the age. Count the number of whorls above chest height and add one year.

COUNT THE GAPS

Count the number of gaps between branch sections, including the section at breast height, and above the last branch.

MEASURE THE CIRCUMFERENCE

Measure the circumference of the trunk about 5 ft (1.5 m) above the ground. Calculate the radius (distance from center of the tree to its outer edge) using the formula $r = C/2\Pi$ (i.e., divide the circumference by 6.283). Then divide the radius by the average yearly tree growth for your tree species (available online) to find its age.

COLLECT, FILTER, AND PURIFY WATER

Collecting water and making it safe
to drink is one of the most important survival skills.

A human being can survive for several weeks without food, but barely three days without water. One of the best ways to collect water (without relying on the rain) is to construct an evaporation trap.

HOW TO MAKE AN EVAPORATION TRAP

You will need some plastic sheeting, a digging tool, a 1¾-pint (1-liter) container, a drinking tube (optional), and some rocks.

- First find a moist area that receives sunlight for most of the day. Dig a bowl-shaped hole about 3 ft 3 in (1 m) in diameter and about 2 ft (60 cm) deep.

- Dig a hole the width of your container in the middle of the floor of the hole and sink the container into it.

- If you have a drinking tube, place one end in the container and the other end outside the hole.

- Place the plastic sheeting over the hole, trap the edges with rocks and then place a single rock in the center of the sheeting so that it forms an inverted cone. Then seal the edges of the sheeting with soil so air cannot escape from the hole.

During the day, the heat of the sun will make the moisture in the ground evaporate into the air, but it will condense again when it hits the plastic sheeting, and this condensed water will drip down the inside of the sheeting and collect in the container. A large trap should produce about 1¾ pints (1 liter) of clean water a day.

HOW TO FILTER WATER

Fill a container (hollow log, plastic bag) with alternating layers of rock, sand, and cloth. Make about ten small holes in the bottom of the container and place an empty container underneath. Then pour water into the top of the filter. This process will remove grit and sediment (a filter made solely of cloth will only remove visible particles). If possible, allow the water to sit for twelve hours after being filtered, to improve the taste.

HOW TO PURIFY WATER

The best way to purify water is to boil it for at least ten minutes. Alternatively, let the water sit for at least six to eight hours in full sunlight. The ultraviolet light will kill most microorganisms.

MAKE A DUGOUT CANOE

If you can only spare a couple of days, use a chainsaw, but if you have a month to burn, why not try the traditional Native American method of using fire as the main tool to hollow out your canoe?

1. Locate and chop down a pine tree with a trunk base that is completely straight, at least 20 ft (6 m) long and about 3 ft (90 cm) in diameter (you can also use a hardwood such as elm or chestnut). Traditionally you would chop down a tree close to a river and work it into a canoe on the river bank, because there would be no easy way to transport the log somewhere else.

2. Strip the branches and place the trunk on a row of smaller logs so that it can be maneuvered more easily.

3. Remove the bark using a three-quarters ax, spade, or a foot adze.

4. Flatten the top by sawing or chopping parallel lines across the trunk and then chipping away with an ax or adze.

5. Dig a depression under the front and back ends of the log and light a fire in each. The flames will burn the underside of the log so you can chop away the charred wood with an adze to create a sloped bow and stern.

6. Burn fires on top of the log along its length and dig out the charcoal each day to hollow out the inside of the canoe. This will take several days. Protect the sides and other areas that you don't want to burn by splashing them with water or backfilling them with clay and mud.

7. Don't let the fire go out. Keep tending it round the clock and make sure you aren't burning the precious sides. The sides should be about 2 in (5 cm) thick.

8. Once you have created the rough interior, lay smaller targeted fires to burn away areas that are too thick, using rocks to press the fires against the targeted areas, while protecting the areas that are already at the required thickness.

9. Traditionally, clam shells would also be used to create a smooth finish inside and out. Then the wood would be rubbed with animal fat.

10. Drag your 220 lb (100 kg) canoe down to the water for its test launch. The beauty of a dugout is that even though it is less stable than a modern canoe, it won't sink if you capsize, even when filled with water.

Tell the time without a clock

Whether it's day or night, so long as you can see the sun or moon, you can estimate the time to within an hour by observing their position in the sky.

DAYTIME SUN METHOD

1. If you are in the northern hemisphere, face south; if you are in the southern hemisphere, face north. The sun always rises in the east and takes between 10 and 14 hours to travel in an arc across the sky before it sets in the west.

2. For this example, let's assume you are in the northern hemisphere. Facing south, look at the position of the sun, then estimate how many hours of daylight there are today (if it's high summer, you can expect about 14; if it's spring or autumn, about 12, and in winter it will be about 10).

3. Mentally divide the 180-degree sweep of sky into equal parts, according to the number of hours in the day. If it's twelve hours, then there will be six hours on the eastern half and six on the western half.

4. If you know how many hours ago the sun rose, you can then count from sunrise to find the approximate time.

5. The sun should be directly in front of/above you at noon, although this doesn't allow for daylight saving hours. Also, in a country with several time zones, you must allow for your position within the country, either adding or subtracting half an hour.

NIGHTTIME MOON METHOD

1. If you are in the northern hemisphere, face south; if you are in the southern hemisphere, face north. The moon always rises in the east and takes between 10 and 14 hours to travel in an arc across the sky before it sets in the west.

2. For this example, let's assume you are in the northern hemisphere. Facing south, look at the position of the moon, then estimate how many hours of darkness there are tonight (if it's high summer, you can expect about 10; if it's spring or autumn, about 12, and in winter it will be about 14).

3. Mentally divide the 180-degree sweep of sky into equal parts, according to the number of hours in the night. If it's twelve hours, then there will be six hours on the eastern half and six on the western half.

4. If you know how many hours ago the moon rose, you can then count from moonrise to find the approximate time.

5. The moon should be directly in front of/above you at midnight, although this doesn't allow for daylight saving hours. Also, in a country with several time zones, you must allow for your position within the country, either adding or subtracting half an hour.

Build an igloo

An igloo is a shelter built out of snow, which is traditionally associated with the Inuit, but it was predominantly used by people of Canada's Central Arctic and Greenland's Thule area.

Snow is a good insulator, so even if the temperature outside is -49°F (-45°C) the inside temperature can reach 61°F (16°C) from body heat alone.

1. Use a snow saw or large knife to cut your building blocks from an area of compacted snow. Each block should be approximately 16 in (40 cm) high, 8 in (20 cm) wide, and 4 in (10 cm) thick (so the thickness of the igloo walls is 4 in [10 cm]).

2. If you can't find compacted snow, fill a large loaf pan with snow to make your bricks. Bash the pan on the ground to compact the snow and press it down firmly with your hands, then place the pan upside down on the ground and tap the snow brick out as if you were building

a sandcastle. The sloping sides of the pan also provide a ready-made tapered brick edge to allow the bricks to slope inward to form a dome as you build upward.

3. Lay a circle of bricks to form your base, leaving a gap at the downwind side wide enough to crawl through. This will be your entrance. Lay a short corridor of bricks three bricks long leading from the entrance.

4. Fill the gap between bricks with snow, and pat the snow where the bricks meet the ground to form a secure base.

5. Use a knife to angle the top of the first layer of bricks so the outside is slightly higher than the inside. Then add your second layer of bricks, overlapping the first layer so that the end of one brick starts in the middle of a first-layer brick (like building a brick wall). The second layer should slope inward slightly so you can begin to see a dome forming.

6. Repeat Step 5 until you have built several layers and are left with a small, round hole at the top. Also use bricks to put a roof on your entrance corridor.

7. Cut a large tapering circular brick (like a giant bath plug) slightly larger than the top hole to plug the final gap, then fill in all the cracks between the bricks, inside and outside, with snow. Cover the igloo floor with compacted snow to reduce heat loss into the ground.

8. Make several ventilation holes in the roof using a stick. This prevents a potentially fatal buildup of carbon dioxide inside the igloo without losing too much heat.

Gut and clean a fish

This technique works for most fish (except flat fish, which requires a different method). If you have caught the fish yourself, gut and clean it as soon as possible (professional trawler workers do it on the boat, so their catch is ready to sell when they hit the shore).

1. Run the fish under cold running water and then dry it with paper towels. This removes the slime and makes it easier to handle.

2. Use a genuine fillet knife and sharpen it before you begin. Its thin, flexible blade practically shapes itself to whatever you're cutting, making your job much easier.

3. If the fish has large scales, remove them, because they can harbor bacteria and get stuck in your teeth. Run the back of the knife along the fish's body. If the scales are quite large, some of them will come away, indicating that the fish needs complete descaling (if the scales don't detach, they can be left alone). Keep scraping with the back of the knife to remove all the scales.

4. If you want to skin the fish, split the skin down the fish's back, loosen the area around the fins, and then peel away using pliers.

5. Place the fish flat on a chopping board, with the belly facing you. Press firmly on the fish with your free hand to stop it from moving, while making a slit from underneath the chin all the way along the belly, between the dorsal fins to the anal fin.

6. Remove the guts. Make sure you remove the brownish-red line that runs along the spine (the kidney line).

7. If you want to keep the head, remove the gills. Remove the head by lifting up the pectoral fin and then cut underneath it using an angled incision toward the head, stopping at the backbone. Repeat on the other side of the head and then cut through the backbone by placing your knife on it and applying pressure. Then cut through any remaining soft tissue that joins the head to the body.

8. To remove the dorsal fin, cut along it on either side then pull the fin away with a sharp pull from the tail end outward.

9. Wash the fish again, inside and out, in cold running water. Clean and sharpen your knife.

Pan for gold

Gold panning is a skillful process that is used to separate small flecks and nuggets of gold from the surrounding sand, gravel, and dirt. When performed correctly, any gold sinks to the bottom of the pan where the base meets the side, where it can be recovered.

1. Fill your pan about three-quarters of the way to the top with gravel, and then find a place on the riverbank where the water is at least 6 in (15 cm) deep. If possible, find a rock to sit on while you pan, as this is less tiring than squatting.

2. First, submerge the pan and use your fingers to break up clods of earth and allow the contents of the pan to become saturated. Some mud and silt will wash away. Don't remove any of the larger stones yet unless they are totally clean, otherwise you may throw away a nugget stuck to a stone.

3. Keeping the pan submerged, shake the contents from left to right; this breaks up the material even more and allows the heavier gold to sink to the bottom.

4. Sweep any clean rocks out of the pan with your hand, or raise the pan out of the water and tilt it down slightly away from your body to allow the water to pour out of the forward edge, taking the top and lightest layer of deposits away with it.

5. Scoop up a little more water and repeat steps 3 and 4 for several minutes until eventually you will be left with about half a cupful of the heaviest materials such as black sand and iron gravel (these are usually the darkest materials, apart from the shiny gold).

6. Use a magnet to remove the magnetic deposits (like the iron). Then add half a cup of water, tilt the pan forward, and shake from left to right, so the black material collects in the forward-bottom of the pan with any gold sinking to the bottom. Level the pan as you swirl in a slow, circular movement, to gradually brush away the concentrates to reveal the gold.

7. Use tweezers or wet fingers to collect specks of gold and place them in your sample pan or collecting bottle. Alternatively, place the entire remaining contents of the pan into a larger collecting jar for further sifting when you get home; this allows you to collect more gold on site, rather than waste precious panning time.

SHOE  HORSE

Wild horses have toughened hooves so they don't need shoes, but domesticated horses require new shoes every four to eight weeks to protect their feet.

These instructions are for information only. The first time you shoe a horse do it under the supervision of an experienced farrier.

1. Gently pat the horse's rump so that it doesn't get startled, then gently run your hand down the leg, squeeze the tendon above the ankle, raise the hoof off the ground, and clamp it between your knees.

2. Remove the old shoe by straightening the nail clinches in the hoof wall using a clinch cutter and a hammer (a bit like picking the staples out of a sheet of paper). Then remove the shoe with a pair of metal pull-offs and a toe-to-heel rocking motion.

3. Use a hoof pick to remove compacted dirt from the bottom of the hoof to create a clean surface. Scrape downward from heel to toe and be aware that the frog—the triangular middle of the hoof—is a sensitive area.

4. Use a hoof knife to remove loose and flaky material from the sole and then use a rasp to make the bottom of the sole smooth and level, ready to receive the shoe.

5. Make minor adjustments to the shoe by heating it and shaping it with hammer and anvil until the shoe aligns with the edge of the hoof.

6. Attach the shoe by driving nails through the holes in the shoe into the edge of the hoof, through the soles at an outward angle, so the tip of the nail eventually pokes out of the hoof wall. Never angle the nails inward, otherwise you will injure the sensitive inner part of the hoof (like driving a nail under your own fingernail).

7. Use the claw end of a hammer to bend the nail tips against the hoof wall, then clip off the tips with metal nippers to leave about ⅛ in (3 mm) of the tip bent over the hole.

8. Place a clinch block under the nail on the hoof wall, then clinch the nail down tight with a driving hammer.

9. Clip and file any excess hoof that is sticking over the edge of the shoe.

10. File the hoof wall to smooth out the clinched nail tips and any rough and uneven patches until you can brush a cloth over the hoof wall without snagging it.

MOUNT *and* DISMOUNT *a horse*

The first thing a rider learns is how to mount and dismount. It is important to get this right, because a poor technique can make the horse edgy and may cause injury to horse or rider.

HOW TO MOUNT

1. Before mounting, check that the girth is tight (otherwise the saddle will slip) and that both stirrups are down.

2. Use a mounting block positioned no more than 20 in (50 cm) from the horse, unless you can comfortably reach the stirrups from the ground. This puts less strain on the horse's back and makes mounting easier and safer for you.

3. Stand at the left side of the horse, holding the reins in your left hand. Grip a bit of mane with your left hand or hold onto the front of the saddle.

4. Place your weight on your right leg and step into the left stirrup with your left foot, with the ball of your foot at the bottom (turn the stirrup with your right hand first if necessary).

5. Transfer your weight onto your left foot and then swing your right leg over the back of the saddle (the cantle), being careful not to kick the horse with either foot.

6. Sit in the saddle, immediately put your right foot in its stirrup and take the reins in both hands, inside your closed fists with your thumb folded over.

HOW TO DISMOUNT

1. Make sure the horse isn't pointing toward its home/paddock, etc., otherwise it could run off early while you are trying to dismount.

2. Remove both feet from the stirrups. Don't be tempted to keep your left foot in the stirrup because this places too much strain on the horse's back and risks your foot being trapped if the horse bolts.

3. Hold the reins in your left hand and place your left hand on the pommel. Lean forward and slide off the horse while bringing your right leg over its back, then land with bent knees to cushion the landing.

4. Slide the left stirrup up the leather so that it doesn't bash against the horse's flanks, then remove your reins from over the horse's head, walk around in front of him to the right stirrup and slide this one up.

SHEAR a SHEEP

The most widely used method of sheep shearing is called the New Zealand shearing pattern.

An experienced shearer works quickly, using a precise sequence of "blows" and moves. The shearer holds the sheep correctly to keep the animal as relaxed as possible while removing the fleece in once piece, shearing as close to the body as possible. These instructions are for information only. The first time you shear a sheep do it under the supervision of an experienced shearer.

1. Don't feed the sheep the day before shearing. This minimizes the amount of waste it produces and keeps your work area clean. Make sure the sheep is clean and dry. Don't shear a wet sheep (this risks electric shock from the shears, and wet wool cannot be rolled and sold).

2. Catch the sheep around the neck and firmly place it on its rump, so that it is sitting between your legs.

3. Starting high on the brisket (breast bone), make five passes down the belly to the open flank, working from top to bottom and left to right. Use your left hand to smooth out wrinkles.

4. Cover the teats with your left hand, then shear the inside of each hind leg and the crotch.

5. While stretching the skin with your left hand, make three blows down the outside of the left hind leg: the first blow down and two more up to the flank.

6. Shear the top of the head (the topknot) with three blows (the third goes in under the horn) followed by three blows from leg to shoulder of the left front leg (the third starts under the shoulder).

7. Return to the left hind leg and make three blows from leg to the rump.

8. Make a blow along the left side of the face then lay the sheep on its right side and make two passes above the backbone from the rump to neck and one pass under the backbone.

9. Shear the neck and right side of the face then lay the sheep on its back and make four long blows from rump to neck along its left side.

10. Roll the sheep back up between your legs so you can make two blows along the right side of the back, ending in a full blow around the shoulder.

11. Lift the head onto your knee and complete the neck with six blows running down the right side of the body, followed by the shoulder and the last side.

12. Tie the fleece with paper twine so that it looks fresh and springy with the back, side, and shoulders (the most valuable part) visible.

Send smoke signals

Smoke signals have been used by many cultures to send simple messages over long distances. In Ancient China, soldiers stationed on the Great Wall used smoke signals to transmit warnings of an imminent attack along the wall from tower to tower. The indigenous peoples of North America are famously associated with their use of smoke signals.

Build a fire on high ground where the smoke can more easily be seen. In North American cultures, the position of the fire was also significant; a fire placed half-way up a hill or mountain meant that all was well, while a mountaintop fire signalled danger. Clear the surrounding area of debris so your fire doesn't spread.

When your fire is burning well, cover it with lush green vegetation and grass or any material that will make the fire produce dense white smoke. Two or three large pieces of green brush are ideal and will produce plenty of smoke for several minutes.

Take a wet blanket and place it over the fire, then briefly remove and replace it again, to create a single puff of smoke. Repeat this to create the desired number of puffs. Each number or sequence of puffs will convey a message that has been prearranged by you and your friends. Each tribe would have had its own repertoire of signals, since they could also be seen by their enemies. Here are some possibilities:

- One continuous column of white smoke signals "attention" and that a message is forthcoming. Two fires producing two columns of smoke would signify that you have set camp and intend to stay in this place until further notice. If your camp was well established, it might inform neighboring tribes that all is favorable and quiet.

- One puff: this also means "attention" and tells your neighbors to be alert for the next signal.

- Two puffs: this means "all is well" and there are no immediate threats.

- Three puffs: this means "danger, enemies are approaching" and "an attack is imminent." The Boy Scouts of America also use the three puffs of smoke to convey that something is seriously wrong.

Cure people with leeches and maggots

In the Middle Ages, leeches, maggots, and bloodletting were used for curing most ills from wounds to madness.

Since then they have acquired a reputation as dangerous quackery, but in fact they weren't used as indiscriminately as folklore would have you believe. Their benefits are as valid today as they were hundreds of years ago.

LEECHES

Leeches were used to reduce the pain and swelling caused by blood trapped under the skin due to trauma. The saliva of leeches has anticlotting and anesthetic properties, so popping a few leeches on an area of black and blue, swollen skin would ease blood flow, reduce the swelling, and lessen the risk of a clot traveling elsewhere in the body.

There are about 600 species of leeches but only about 15 of them are used medicinally. They can be used to treat rheumatism, vascular diseases, hypertension, diabetes, gastrointestinal tract problems, lung problems such as bronchitis and bronchial asthma, and skin conditions such as psoriasis and eczema.

1. Wash the subject's foot and then place four medical leeches (*Hirudo medicinalis*) between the toes. Once the leeches have latched on with their jaws (painlessly), they will suck blood for between two and five hours (depending on the person's circulation) and grow to the size of a human thumb.

2. Remove the leech and set aside (it won't need to feed again for another six months).

MAGGOTS

Maggots are used to clean necrotic (dead) tissue from a wound. Infected living tissue cannot heal, so it must be cleaned (debrided) if the patient is to make a full recovery. Not only do the maggots eat dead tissue, but their saliva contains powerful antibacterial agents.

1. Ensure that the wound site is suitable for maggot therapy—a moist exudating wound with an oxygen supply. Dry or open body cavity wounds are not suitable.

2. Only use green blowfly larvae (*Phaenicia sericata*) that have been grown in a laboratory setting so they are sterilized and free from secondary infections. You could also use the species *Protophormia terraenovae*, whose saliva combats certain Streptococcal infections.

3. Apply no more than eight maggots per square half inch (centimeter) of surface in the treatment area. Cover the area with a bandage so they can't escape. Replace the bandage and maggots every two days until the wound is clean.

Keep bees and harvest honey

Beekeeping involves a significant commitment in terms of time, learning, and responsibility.

If you want to keep bees, do proper research and take advice from an expert who can mentor and monitor you while you learn. The instructions that follow are intended as an introduction and not as a substitute for expert training. For more information, contact your local beekeepers' association.

1. Ensure that your garden is large enough to keep bees and that the hive is sufficiently far away from you and your neighbors. You also need to be aware of how much work is involved and the cost. One colony can swallow 50 hours of your time a season, so multiply this by the number of hives. The start-up cost is about $600 (£500) for one hive.

2. The main considerations are which way your hive will face (probably east) and what the bees' main source of food will be. You need to establish a flight path that doesn't adversely affect you or your neighbors. Don't locate your hive close to a footpath or road, or close to a children's playground.

3. Purchase, borrow, or build your own starter hive. There are three main types of hive: the top bar single-story frameless beehive in which the comb hangs from removable bars (rather than frames); the standard Langstroth hive in which the comb hangs from removable frames; and the cedar wood Hex Hive® (created by beekeeper Randy Sue Collins) that more closely resembles the bees' natural tree trunk habitat.

4. You can buy a nucleus of bees from an established beekeeper or use a temporary "swarm box" to capture your own bees naturally for free. Bees swarm around springtime—the colony divides when it gets too big and half the bees follow the queen and find a new place to live. If you see a swarm on a tree, you can cut off the branch and place the swarm in your swarm box, then put some open frames in with some starter honeycomb.

5. Leave the swarm box there all day, then take it home after nightfall and you can add the frames to your hive.

6. You must harvest the surplus honey in a natural and sustainable way, leaving enough honey to support the colony. Many commercial beekeeping operations force nature by harvesting all the honey and then supplementing the bees' diet with sugar water or high fructose corn syrup. This is detrimental to the bee colony; it produces honey that not only lacks the health benefits of organic honey, but is actually bad for you. With effective management, you can expect to harvest 45–65 lb (20–30 kg) of surplus honey from an established hive in its second year.

Pluck a chicken

After wringing the chicken's neck or chopping off the head, hang it upside down to allow the blood to drain away. Then the bird is ready for plucking.

1. Soak the bird in scalding water (between 140 and 150°F [60 and 66°C]) for about 45 seconds to loosen the feathers. Swish the bird around a bit so the water reaches deep into the feathers and quills.

2. Remove from the water and quickly dunk the body in cold water. This prevents the skin from tearing while you pluck.

3. Now simply pluck the feathers using your hands. Use needle-nose pliers to remove any tough feathers or broken quills that are hard to grip. Plucking takes its toll on the fingertips, so always use pliers when the going gets tough, otherwise your hands will become very sore. You can also use a table knife, by gripping the feather between thumb and blade and pulling.

4. Clean and remove internal organs. Slit the skin on top of the neck from the backbone to the end of the neck. Separate the neck from the windpipe and crop, then remove them with your fingers. Cut and discard.

5. Cut the neck off at the backbone and then cut the feet off at the leg joint (cutting through cartilage, not bone).

6. Now, carefully slit the body cavity. Start underneath the breastplate and work your knife around the edge of the carcass underneath the bottom and back around the other side in an ellipse until your knife reaches back where you started. Don't press your knife in too far because piercing the intestines or the bile duct will spoil the taste of the meat.

7. Place your hand into the cavity under the breast bone with your palm facing downward and scoop out the innards. Scrape the cavity to remove any leftovers.

If you want to eat the feet, liver, and gizzard, prepare them as follows:

Feet: Remove the socks. They should peel away; if not, give them another quick soak in the scalding water.

Liver: Remove the bile duct.

Gizzard (the muscular, thick-walled part of a bird's stomach for grinding food): Pry it open and remove all the contents. Then peel off the yellow lining.

MAKE FIRE WITH  BOW DRILL

The bow drill is an ancient tool, dating back thousands of years. It is easy to make and with a little practice, is the most reliable friction fire technique, even in damp weather.

1. Find a curved stick about 2 ft (60 cm) long (or armpit to fingertip length) and thick enough to remain rigid while you are bowing.

2. Turn the stick into a bow by tying a piece of string from one end to the other (a shoelace, rawhide, or natural fiber such as dogbane or milkweed).

3. Make a fireboard from a piece of dry dead wood about 4 in (10 cm) wide, at least ¾ in (2 cm) thick, and at least 8 in (20 cm) long. If digging your thumb into the wood leaves a mark, it's a good piece of wood for fire making. Carve a shallow recess in the wood about 1¼ in (3 cm) from the edge. Cut a V into the edge at this point.

4. Find a top rock, made out of hardwood, rock, bone, or shell that fits comfortably in your hand.

5. Make a spindle using the same type of wood as your fireboard—a straight stick about 1 in (2.5 cm) diameter and about 8 in (20 cm) long, rounded at one end and with the other end carved into a point.

6. Place the spindle into the middle of the bow and twist so that it is caught in a loop. The tension of the string should be such that if you let go the spindle would twist out.

7. If you are right-handed, kneel on your right leg and place your left foot on the left side of the fireboard, in front of and at right angles to your right knee. Hold the bow in your right hand and place the spindle in the hole in the fireboard.

8. Place tinder (material that ignites easily—dry leaves, moss, bark, milkweed fluff, grasses, etc.) into the V.

9. Hold the spindle in place by pressing down hard with your left hand, while bracing your left wrist against your shin.

10. Draw the bow back and forward with your right hand while pressing down hard with your left hand, forcing the point of the spindle into the hole in the fireboard. Start off slowly to conserve your energy; when sufficient sawdust has filled the hole, go fast until it begins to smoke.

11. Stop bowing, remove the fireboard, and gently blow on the sawdust until it ignites your tinder and flames appear.

Learn FLINT KNAPPING

Flint knapping technology is about fifteen times older than our own species, Homo sapiens. The earliest evidence of stone tools dates back more than 3 million years.

A flint knapper shapes stones by striking them with another stone called the hammer stone. Any mineral that leaves a smooth surface after fracture can be knapped, including flint, basalt, obsidian, and lab-manufactured quartz.

1. Select a core stone that has few or no cracks or significant irregularities which will adversely affect the way it flakes.

2. Sit down and place a towel on your left knee. Hold the core in your left hand and support it on your left knee. Hold the hammer stone in your right hand.

3. First you must break off a small piece of flint from your core suitable for further shaping into an arrowhead.

4. Strike the core sharply with the hammer stone with a downward glancing blow with follow-through. The angle between the two surfaces should be less than 90 degrees. Keep striking the edge of the core until a suitable piece flakes off.

5. If your core surface becomes uneven, make a series of smaller strikes to remove little flakes. This prevents the core from crushing when it is struck.

6. To make smaller to medium-sized arrowheads, select a large flake, dress and abrade the edge, and then use pressure flaking.

7. Abrade the edge (this is the most important part of flint knapping). Each time you have struck off a series of flakes on an edge, you must grind the edge down or the whole edge will collapse when you strike it again. Do this by grinding the edge in a sawing motion against another flat stone of slightly lesser hardness.

8. For pressure flaking, hold a piece of leather in your palm (or a concave stone or shell). Place the flint edge on top with the cutting edge facing you and grip it with the flat fingers of your left hand. Then apply long, slow, downward pressure on the edge toward the palm, using a pointed tool (like a blunt bradawl). This will chip a thin flake from one tiny part of the edge. The longer the flakes the better. This is the most time-consuming part of the process and takes about ten times as long as abrading. Don't forget to continue abrading the edge after every series of flakes.

Make a bow from a sapling

Making a usable bow that can catch small animals in a survival situation is time-consuming but fairly straightforward. The bow won't win an Olympic event but it will fire an arrow fast and true enough to be lethal.

1. Cut a straight hardwood sapling about 2½ in (6 cm) thick that is about the same height as you. Split it down the middle using a froe or bowie knife. If you are lucky, you may end up with two usable staves.

2. Using a sharp ax, rasp, or big kitchen knife, whittle down the staff on the inside until it is just over 1 in (2.5 cm) thick with a nice taper at each end. This rough tillering speeds up the wood-seasoning process.

3. Take the staff inside and tie it at several places along its length to something flat and solid like a workbench or bedpost, so that it dries straight. Seal the ends of the staff with some glue. This prevents the staff from cracking as it seasons. Leave it to season for about three weeks (skip this step if you need the bow immediately).

4. Round off the corners and continue the long and patient process of tillering using a rasp to remove more wood from the belly (inside) of the bow, working from handle to tip, so that it tapers to about ½ in (1.25 cm) at each end, leaving a handle about 4 in (10 cm) long and between 1 and 1½ in (2.5 and 4 cm) wide, depending on the size of your hand.

5. Cut a notch about 2 in (5 cm) from each end and string the bow, so that you can draw the string and see how the bow is bending. As you work, keep testing the bend by flexing the bow and then removing wood from areas where the bend is stiff; then tighten the string and test again.

6. You should end up with a bow that bends uniformly with no weak spots that are too thin or stiff spots that are too thick. Toward the end, stop using the rasp and switch to different grades of sandpaper. When you are satisfied that the bow bends in a uniform curve and you have sanded to the desired finish, rub with some linseed oil.

7. Finally, string the bow to full tension, wrap some duct tape, leather, or cloth around the handle to make it more comfortable to hold, and your bow is ready to use.

MAKE AND FLETCH AN ARROW

Arrows are very expensive to buy, but it is possible to make cheap and reasonably effective arrows yourself from a dowel rod and duct tape from the hardware store.

1. Buy a ½ in (1 cm) oak dowel rod. Make a slit (nock) in one end using a saw blade from a multi-tool or a small hacksaw. The nock fits into the string when you fire the arrow. The nock has to be wide enough to sit on the string well but not so tight that you split the dowel. You can use a file to widen the nock until it fits well.

2. Whittle the sides of the dowel so the nock fits between the two nock points on your bow string.

3. Now you are ready to put some duct tape "feathers" on the shaft. Turn the dowel so the nock is horizontal.

4. Attach a 4 in (10 cm) piece of duct tape along the shaft just below the nock and about half the diameter of the arrow. Then attach another piece opposite it on the other side of the shaft, so the adhesive sides are facing each other. Starting at the shaft, press the two pieces of tape together, being careful not to get any ridges or wrinkles.

5. Do the same thing with two more pieces of tape to make a rectangle on the opposite side of the shaft.

6. Using a sharp knife or pair of scissors, cut each rectangle into a triangle, wide at the end and tapering into the shaft further down.

7. Construct two more rectangular flaps of duct tape each at a 90-degree angle to your first two feathers and then cut them to the same triangular shape to form a four-fletched arrow.

8. To figure out how long your arrow needs to be, hold the nock end against the corner of your mouth as if you were drawing it on an imaginary bow. Support the other end of the arrow with your other hand, arm extended as if it were holding the bow. Stick your index finger out on the arrow and the tip of your index finger is where the tip of the arrow needs to be.

9. Cut the end off and taper it down with a knife, like sharpening a pencil, then you can attach a glue-on broad head.

BUILD AND USE  A PIT OVEN

Whether you are camping or just want to try something different in your own yard, a pit oven cooks food slowly and evenly and adds a satisfying frontier flavor that you just don't get with a conventional domestic oven.

1. Dig the hole well away from overhanging vegetation, dry brush, or other flammable hazards. Unless you plan to roast a whole boar, a smallish hole with vertical walls roughly 2 ft (60 cm) by 3 ft (90 cm) by 1 ft (30 cm) deep is sufficient. The hole needs to be roughly three times the size of the food you are cooking. Pile the dirt nearby as you'll need it later.

2. Line the pit with stones and pebbles. Use flat stones for the sides and bottom of the hole and then pile a few rounder stones in the base of the hole, which also give extra support to the side stones and stop them from falling down. Don't use rocks from the bottom of a river as they tend to explode when the water inside them turns to steam.

3. Build a fire inside the hole. Start with scrunched-up newspapers, then place kindling such as twigs and dry moss on top, followed by charcoal and thicker logs.

4. Light the fire and keep it burning for at least an hour to heat the stones, then rake over the embers so that the heat spreads evenly over all the stones.

5. Wrap your fish, meat, potatoes, or whatever you want to cook in thick baking foil to keep it clean while it cooks, or if you want to be more traditional, wrap it in large, edible leaves or fresh grass. Large joints of meat can be cut into smaller squares to ensure they cook properly; if you are cooking a whole chicken, you can place a few hot stones inside the body cavity.

6. Place a layer of foil/fresh grass/edible leaves on top of the stones. Then place the food packages on top (most people prefer to remove the embers or scrape them to one side because if they are too hot they will burn the food).

7. Lay down a couple of layers of foil/leaves on top of the food and then fill the hole with dirt.

8. Leave the food to cook slowly for about two hours, then dig the dirt out and carefully rescue your meal, being careful not to pierce the food covering with your spade. Be very careful, since the stones will still be hot enough to give you a nasty burn.

9. After you've finished, fill in the hole and the oven will be protected until the next time you want to cook with it.

CHOP DOWN A TREE WITH AN AX

Chopping down a tree with an ax is really hard work, especially if you don't know what you're doing. It's also very dangerous, so before you even make the first chop, follow this checklist.

PREPARATION

1. Choose the right size ax for the job. The two most important factors are the weight of the cutting head and the length of the haft (the wooden shaft). Choose the longest haft and heaviest head that you can comfortably handle (this will depend on your strength and height—a short person may struggle with a long haft). A typical felling ax weighs about 3½ lb (1.6 kg). The heavier the head and longer the haft, the greater the leverage and cutting power.

2. Sharpen the ax so that it is sharp enough to whittle wood, like a knife. Check that the head is securely attached to the haft and that the haft is not cracked.

3. Clear vegetation and other obstructions from around the tree so you have a clear range of movement.

4. Decide where you want the tree to fall and then plan an escape route. Do not stand behind a falling tree, as the end may kick back and injure you.

5. Wear gloves and safety goggles and work with a friend, in case of injury.

6. Warm up. Swing your arms and do some stretches. Wielding an ax puts a lot of strain on your back.

CUTTING THE TREE

1. Cut a kerf (notch) into the side on which you want the tree to fall using 45-degree-angle chops, alternating between top and bottom of the wedge. Continue until the kerf is about one-third of the way into the trunk.

2. If the kerf is too narrow and you keep trapping your ax, cut a new one above the first and split this piece off to widen the kerf.

3. Cut a second kerf slightly above the first on the opposite side of the trunk. Extend this until it is a little more than halfway through the trunk.

4. You should be left with a small offset of wood that acts as a hinge when the tree falls and should stop the end from kicking back.

5. If the tree begins to lean in the wrong direction, put a wedge in the second kerf and then drive the block to push the tree over.

Thatch a roof

Thatching is one of the oldest surviving traditional building crafts and dates back 4,500 years to the Bronze Age.

It takes about five years' apprenticeship to perfect the skills required, and thatching is very labor-intensive (and expensive). A thatched roof only lasts for about forty years.

1. Traditionally, the most common thatching material was wheat or rye straw, which were a by-product of grain production. The best thatching straw is "long straw"—tall, strong-stemmed straw grown from older wheat varieties without fertilizer, which makes the straw less durable.

2. Use a reaper-binder to harvest the straw before the stem is fully ripened (otherwise it will become brittle). Tie the straw into bundles and leave it "shocked" in the field for two weeks to dry out before threshing to remove the grain.

3. After threshing, prepare the straw for thatching by laying it on the ground and dousing it with a little water so that handfuls of straw can be drawn out and tied into neat clumps called "yelms"—about 4¼ in (13 cm) thick and 17¾ in (45 cm) in breadth.

4. Begin thatching at the eaves of one end of the roof. Lay a yelm on the roof with the flower ends facing up the roof. Temporarily holding it in place with iron thatching pins, clip the binding off the bundle.

5. Use a legget (which looks like a flat aluminum spade) to dress the thatch: beat the butt ends so that they form a smooth, uniform surface.

6. Permanently fix the yealm in place by hammering large spiked hooks called thatching crooks through the yelm into the wooden rafter beneath. The crook hooks onto a hazel rod or steel sway which runs horizontally across the yealms to keep them in place. Remove the thatching pins.

7. Take another yelm, wedge it against the first, and repeat the process to fix it to the roof. When you have four or five yelms in place, work in strips from eave to apex, with each course of straw overlapping the one below. Aim for a minimum 14 in (35 cm) depth of thatch.

8. Once applied, comb the thatch with a large "side rake" to remove short or loose straw and to line up all the surface straws vertically.

9. When both sides of the roof have been thatched, ridge the apex by butting up material on both sides. A simple flush ridge is the most resilient, while an ornamental pattern may look impressive but increases the risk of water leaking into the core of the thatch because of a misplaced spar.

10. Cover the roof with wire netting to protect it from the birds.

CLIMB A LADDER
safely

75°

Every year tens of thousands of people seriously injure themselves by falling off ladders. So either humans have forgotten how to use this relatively modern invention or else they have never really mastered it at all.

Follow these tips if you want to avoid becoming another statistic.

CHOOSE YOUR LADDER

1. Always choose the correct ladder for the job in terms of height and weight-bearing ability. Ladders have weight ratings. Check the rating to ensure the ladder suits the task.

2. An extension ladder should extend a few rungs higher than you need to reach, and step ladders should allow you to reach your target without having to stand on the very top.

3. Do not allow the ladder to stick up more than 3 feet (90 cm) above its upper support.

4. Always check the condition of the ladder before use. Look for cracks, broken or missing rungs, loose nails or screws, and splinters.

5. Never place the ladder on a box or use any other means of gaining extra height. If the ladder is too short, get a longer one.

PLACEMENT

1. An extension ladder should be placed against a wall at a 75-degree angle. This means that the distance between the bottom rung and the wall is one-quarter of the vertical height. If the angle is any steeper than this, the ladder could fall backward; if the angle is greater, the ladder could slip away at the bottom, and you could overload it.

2. If you have to climb onto another surface at the top of the ladder, such as a roof, allow a few feet of ladder to stick out above the roof, so that you can grip the sides.

3. Make sure the bottom of the ladder is placed on solid, horizontal ground. If you have no choice but to rest it on a slope, wedge a wide piece of wood underneath one of the sides until it is level and secure.

4. Do not lean your ladder against a window or gutter. Make sure that both of the top ends are supported. Where possible, avoid using the top rung as a support (e.g., wedging it against a pole). If you must do this, tie foam padding around the rung to prevent it from slipping.

5. Where possible, always tie off the ladder at the top so that it can't slip.

CLIMBING UP AND DOWN

1. Face the ladder and use both hands.

2. Place your hands on the side of the ladder and climb one rung at a time, placing your feet in the center of the rungs.

3. Do not carry heavy tools or other equipment in your hands. Either wear a tool belt, or raise the equipment on a rope once you are securely placed at the top.

4. One of the major causes of ladder accidents is overextending. When leaning sideways, your waist should always stay within the sides of the ladder. Always move the ladder rather than reach too far.

5. Do not climb above the point of support, as this could lever the base of the ladder away from the ground.

USE A SCYTHE

A scythe is a great tool for cutting high grass that is overgrown or in places where the ground is uneven or inaccessible for a lawn mower.

It's physical work, but it gets you in contact with the earth and is very satisfying once you've learned the correct technique.

1. Before you start, sharpen the blade with a whetstone. Work from the heel of the blade toward the toe, making a series of downward strokes with the whetstone on the back of the blade. Then repeat the action on the front of the blade to remove any burrs.

2. Grasp the scythe handles so that the blade is on your right, your right hand on the lower handle, and your left hand on the upper handle.

3. Place the blade on the ground and throughout the stroke, keep the blade on the ground and use the same angle. Stand up straight and, keeping your feet on the ground, make a twisting motion to the left to cut the grass, keeping the blade close to the ground.

4. Bring the blade back to the starting position and then twist again to the left to make another cut, stepping forward or backward between cuts to reach new grass.

SALT-CURE meat

Curing is a traditional way of preserving meat, usually by adding salt. Before refrigeration it was the primary way to prolong the life of meat. Pork and beef are the meats most usually associated with curing: The first method is a dry-cure pork belly and the second is a brine beef recipe.

DRY-CURE PORK BELLY

1. Buy 5 lb (2.3 kg) of fresh pork belly from your local butcher. Wash and trim as necessary.

2. Make the salt and season rub by mixing 2 oz (50 g) of salt, 2 tsp of pink curing salt, 4 tbsp of black pepper, 3 bay leaves, 1 tsp of nutmeg, 6 oz (175 g) of brown sugar, 5 crushed cloves of garlic, 4 sprigs of thyme, and 4 sprigs of rosemary.

3. Coat the meat with the mixture so that both sides are well covered.

4. Cover the meat with greaseproof paper, place into an airtight plastic bag, and leave in the refrigerator for 3 days. Then remove

the juices that have leaked out of the meat into the bag, cover the pork in more rub, and leave in the refrigerator for another 4 days.

5. Remove the belly from the refrigerator and roll it up. Use butcher's twine to tie it together, crisscrossing several times as you work along the belly.

6. Air dry the meat by hanging it in a dry room with good air circulation at 60°F (15°C) for 3 or 4 weeks.

7. Rinse the pork belly with cold water to wash off all the seasonings.

SALT BEEF BRISKET

1. Fill a large saucepan with 2 liters of water, 1.1 lb (500 g) of sea salt, 14 oz (400 g) of demerara sugar, ½ oz (15 g) of saltpeter, 6 bay leaves, 6 cloves, a bunch of thyme, and 3 tsp of black peppercorns. Bring to boil, stirring to dissolve the soluble ingredients. Boil for five minutes and leave to cool to room temperature.

2. Pour the brine solution into a nonmetallic container and add a 5½ lb (2.5 kg) beef brisket that has been pricked all over. Make sure it is completely covered. Leave the container in the refrigerator for seven days.

3. Remove the brisket from the brine solution and rinse in cold water, then braise with some chopped carrots, onion, celery sticks, and rosemary for 3 hours until tender.

Ride an
ANTIQUE BICYCLE

The early bicycle, or "penny-farthing," was invented in 1871 in Britain. It was named for the smallest and largest coins in circulation at the time because of the contrast in size between the two wheels.

The large wheel was necessary because the pedals were connected to it directly. Riding one of these magnificent old bikes is easy, but mounting and dismounting is quite a challenge.

1. Stand behind the bicycle and hold the handlebars. Place your left foot on the mounting peg, which is attached to the main body above the back wheel.

2. Looking straight ahead, push off briskly with your other foot so the bike moves forward with enough speed for you to climb onto the seat.

3. Briefly stand on the mounting peg with both feet, before sliding into the seat.

4. Before you lose speed, as the pedal reaches the top of its revolution, catch it with your foot and push down and then catch the other pedal with the other foot and start pedalling.

5. Pedal smoothly, maintaining a steady pace and focusing at least 15 ft (4.5 m) in front of you.

6. Don't look down but stay alert for obstacles such as potholes and stones that can be treacherous when riding such an ungainly vehicle.

7. Turn the handlebars to steer but sit upright and don't lean into the turns like you would with a modern bike.

8. To dismount, pedal backward while applying the brakes. Moving in a straight line, keep looking forward and throw your left foot back onto the mounting step but don't look down at your feet.

9. With your left foot on the mounting step, slide out of the seat, bending your left leg, so that your right leg can touch the ground if the bike falls over.

10. Bring the bike to a controlled stop, then dismount fully by placing your left foot on the ground, and release the handlebars.

Survive a bear attack

If you are attacked by a bear, the odds are definitely stacked against you, since one swipe can kill and its powerful jaws can crush your head like an egg.

However, if you stay calm, assess the situation, and act quickly and decisively, you can increase your chances of survival.

1. First assess whether the animal is acting defensively (in which case it is potentially less of a threat, although still very dangerous) or if it wants to eat you (in which case you're in the greatest danger). A defensive bear may be protecting its cubs or a supply of food, or be startled by your arrival. A hungry predatory bear will actively seek you out.

2. A bear makes a defensive attack by trying to swat you and bite your body rather than your head or neck, or the animal may make a series of bluff charges. If charged, stand still since you won't be able to outrun the bear. After a defensive bluff attack, wave your arms slowly above your head and back away slowly, talking softly. A defensive bear will be less likely to follow after you cease to be a threat.

3. A bear makes a predatory attack by swinging the head from side to side and gnashing teeth, biting your neck and the top of your head, or grasping you in a bear hug. Even if you escape, you will be pursued.

4. Stay calm. Make yourself look as large as possible, by spreading your arms and legs. Leave your backpack on (it may afford some protection). Avoid eye contact but don't turn your back.

5. Some people have scared away bears by bashing metallic objects. However, this may also attract the bear. Your best bet is to stay quiet and avoid any sudden movements. Back away slowly, but don't run, as this will trigger the bear's pursuit instinct.

6. Grizzly bears are worse climbers than black bears, but the general rule is don't climb a tree. Bears can climb trees better than you, and a predatory bear will follow you up a tree (unless you can climb to the topmost branches that won't support the bear's weight).

7. If the bear makes physical contact, use whatever you can find (sticks, rocks) to attack. Throw dirt or poke a stick/knife into its eyes, or throw objects at its face. Hit the sensitive snout squarely with a rock or fist. Perform a quick and powerful straight-line kick to the gut.

8. If you are injured, playing dead will not deter a predatory bear, although it might disarm a defensive attack.

Survive an avalanche

If you are caught in an avalanche, there are a some things you can do to either escape being hit by it or to increase your chance of survival if you become buried.

1. If you have triggered the avalanche yourself and the snow begins to collapse under your feet, if you react quickly enough you may be able to jump up the slope above the fracture line where the avalanche began. It's a long shot but this has been done.

2. Ditch your nonessential equipment such as skis and backpack (keep your snow shovel and avalanche beacon and probe). If you get hit you want to be as light and mobile as possible.

3. Start running sideways to the edge of the flow (even if the avalanche is below you). The snow travels the fastest in the center of the avalanche, and the volume of snow is the highest here, so if you reach the sides you stand a better chance and you may even escape it altogether.

4. If there is a sturdy tree nearby that you can hug, grip onto it. An avalanche can rip away trees but you may be able to hold on.

5. If the snow covers you, start swimming upward—kicking with your legs and paddling with your hands, to stop your body from sinking. Swim uphill and on your back so that your face is uppermost if you get buried.

6. If you are getting completely buried, raise your hand straight in the air so that when you come to a halt you will know which way is up. Cup your other hand or arm over your face to create an air pocket. You may be lucky enough to have a hand or arm poking above the surface, making it easier for rescuers to spot you. Another way to check which way is down is to dribble saliva. If it rolls down your chin you know you are upright; if it rolls into your nose, you are upside down.

7. Once the snow stops flowing, if you are buried by more than a foot of snow you won't be able to get out. Dig an air pocket near your hand and mouth and take a deep breath before the snow settles. This means that when you exhale you will have some room for your chest to expand and contract.

8. Don't waste oxygen by struggling to escape or yelling for help (unless you know that rescuers are nearby). Keep calm and wait patiently to be rescued.

9. If you need to urinate, do so. The smell will help tracker dogs to locate you.

SURVIVE A FOREST FIRE

Every year, wildfires destroy thousands of acres of vegetation, drive people out of their homes, consume houses and agricultural land, devastate communities, and kill. They spread quickly and can reach temperatures exceeding 1,000°F (540°C).

1. The best protection is to leave the area. Wildfires are powerful and unpredictable, so if you are advised to evacuate, do so; otherwise, you could be putting other people's lives at risk, not just your own.

2. While you are waiting for the local government or media broadcasts to tell you to evacuate, plan an escape route and be aware of safe zones such as rivers or open spaces that you can reach if you are unable to completely escape the conflagration.

3. If it is a large fire, you will hear the flames before you see them, and you will observe the local wildlife fleeing.

4. Figure out which way the wind is blowing and move laterally to this. The fire will spread in the direction of the wind. Try also to get below the line of the fire as quickly as possible. Fire races uphill. Look for a downhill escape route but avoid canyons or gulleys as these will funnel the deadly heat from the fire below directly at you.

5. If superheated air currents from the flames are rushing toward you, try to find a ditch or hollow or large outcroppings of rocks. Stay low and breathe inside your clothing to protect your lungs from the hot gases.

6. An area that has already been razed to the ground by fire may provide refuge, but the ground may still be too hot to bear. You should remain alert to the danger of damaged trees falling on you.

7. If you are above a fire and can reach the ridge of a mountain quickly, you may be able to scramble safely down the other side. Once the fire has crossed the ridge, it will spread more slowly down the mountain.

8. If you are in a vehicle and the fire catches up to you or traps you, close the windows and ventilation panels, leave the engine running, and stay in the vehicle (unless it is a convertible with a fabric roof). Get down on the floor. As long as the petrol tank doesn't explode, the car will provide better protection than running headlong into the flames. As soon as the fire front has passed, try to drive away or else flee the vehicle immediately.

BUILD A *coracle*

A coracle is a small, lightweight, portable boat, usually suitable for one person. made of tar-covered material or hide stretched over a wooden frame, It is one of the oldest and simplest boats, and may date back as far as the Early Bronze Age.

1. First make a seat by cutting a plank of wood 1¼ in (3 cm) thick, 10 in (25 cm) wide, and 3ft 3 in (1 m) long. Drill two holes in each end about 6 in (15 cm) apart.

2. Cut down about 60 willow stakes, at least 6 ft 6 in (2 m) long. Work with them while they are fresh and flexible.

3. Place the seat flat on the ground (a lawn or field of short grass is a good place to work). Stake about 35 willow rods vertically into the

ground about 8 in (20 cm) apart to form an oval shape around the seat. Two rods go through each end of the seat.

4. Weave three rows (each two willows thick) around the bottom of the stakes to form the bottom of the edge of the coracle.

5. Bend the willow stakes on the short sides over to the other side, tie them with twine to their opposite number, and stick the ends into the opposite edge.

6. Bend the willow stakes on the long sides over to their opposite number, and weave them through the willows that run across them. Stick the ends into the opposite edge.

7. Take the coracle out of the ground. Weave three rows (each two willows thick) around the top of the seat edge then cut off the ends of the stakes so they are flush with the edge.

8. Your frame is complete. It should be strong enough for you to kneel on the overturned hull and bounce up and down. Each strut of the frame should consist of two stakes side by side because in Steps 5 and 6 you bent each stake over to meet its counterpart.

9. Now stretch a large piece of calico over the outside of the frame, wrap the ends over the edge of the coracle and sew it where it meets the edge.

10. Make the coracle watertight by applying three coats of tar paint to the outside surface, leaving at least a week between each coat to allow the paint to dry.

Save yourself from drowning

If you are either swept out to sea or have to abandon a sinking ship, your main priorities should be conserving energy and body heat so that you can stay alive for as long as possible to maximize your chances of being rescued.

In cold water the rate at which your body cools depends on a number of factors, including body size, body fat, age, gender, shivering response, water and air temperature, wind, your clothing, and whether you are wearing a PFD (personal flotation device).

In water that is below 50°F (10°C), your survival time is about three hours. The predicted survival time for an average-sized, lightly clothed adult in 50°F (10°C) water is:

Without PFD

Drown proofing	1.5 hours
Treading water	2 hours

With PFD

Swimming	2 hours
Holding still	2.7 hours
H.E.L.P. position	4 hours
Huddle with others	4 hours

1. Get as much of your body out of the water as possible. Climb onto an overturned hull or a piece of driftwood. If none is available, hug a smaller floating object to increase your buoyancy.

2. Keep your clothes on.

3. Don't try to swim to safety unless there is no chance of being rescued and the shore is less than a mile away.

4. Use drown-proofing, H.E.L.P. techniques, and the huddle position to conserve energy.

DROWN PROOFING (WITHOUT PFD)

This survival technique was developed by swimming coach Fred Lanoue during the 1940s. It involves floating in a near vertical position, with the top of the head just above the water surface, keeping the lungs fully inflated for maximum buoyancy. The head is raised only to take a rapid breath. It is the best way to remain afloat with the minimum effort, although if you have a PFD, you should use the H.E.L.P. position instead.

H.E.L.P. (WITH PFD)

This Heat Escape Lessening Posture protects the core areas of the body (head and neck, sides of chest, armpits, and groin) from rapid heat loss.

- Keep your head out of the water and lean back against the collar of your life jacket.

- Fold your arms across your chest and hug the jacket close to your body.

- Press your upper arms against your body so your armpits are closed tight.

- Cross your legs below the knees, press them together and bring them up toward your chest.

HUDDLE POSITION (WITH PFD)

With two or more people, huddle together with arms around each other's waist or shoulders, chests touching and wrap legs around each other. Children should go into the middle of the group, where they will gain the greatest protection.

Tie a hangman's noose

Apart from its more sinister function, the hangman's noose is a useful way to tie the end of a rope securely around an object, regardless of its size.

Never place a noose around your or someone else's neck, even as a joke.

1. Form the end of the rope into an "S" shape and hold these two loops in your left hand, so you are holding three thicknesses of rope, leaving about 2 ft (60 cm) of rope in your right hand (the top of the S).

2. Make a third loop by bringing your right hand (the top end of the S) counterclockwise and then down behind the S and up around the front to form a shamrock shape.

3. Wrap the end of the rope in your right hand around the right and top leaves/loops of the shamrock several times (the traditional hangman's noose has thirteen coils, but eight will suffice).

4. Gently pull it tight so the top loop tightens to form one of the noose loops and then when you have made all your noose loops, feed the remaining rope through the left-hand leaf/loop of the shamrock and pull tight.

5. Tighten the noose to the required length by holding the coil and pulling against the main length of rope.

6. To untie the knot, pull the loop all the way through the coil.

Track animals

Every living creature leaves clues in its environment that reveal a mass of information about itself and its behavior and motivation.

Knowing where to find animals in their habitat involves tracking these clues—a skill known as "sign tracking." Trackers look for large, medium, and small signs.

LARGE

The largest signs are found by reading the landscape itself and understanding how different types of landscape support different species or behavior within a species (e.g., distinguishing between a travel route, a feeding area, and a sleeping place). Most animal life is concentrated in pockets, with little in between. For example, if you were tracking deer you wouldn't expect to see them milling around in an open field. You could go deep into a forest where there is good cover from predators, but a deer here would be difficult to spot. The best place to see deer (indeed many animals) are the transition areas between two types of habitat—forest and field, field and stream, or lakes where the trees come right down to the water line and offer excellent cover.

MEDIUM

Some important medium-scale signs include:

Rub: places where animals rub against an object such as a branch and leave behind hair/feathers, or they might wallow in mud to remove parasites.

Gnaws and chews: teeth marks, leaves and branches that have been bitten off. The way this has been done gives you clues about the animal responsible. For example, a deer would leave jagged shredding damage on a branch because it has no incisors in the upper front part of its jaws.

Broken branches: give you clues about the height of the animal and the way the vegetation has responded gives you a timeline.

Scat: a mine of information. The size, shape, and consistency can help you distinguish between a fox and raccoon, rabbit or deer (often confused).

- Thick, tube-shaped: dog, raccoon, skunk, opossum, wolverine, and bear
- Tubular and tapered at both ends: fox
- Ends in teardrop: cat family
- Wide thread shape: weasel family
- Tiny and round: rabbits and hares
- Tiny and elliptical (pill shaped): deer
- Long and thin: rodents
- Bird droppings: tend to be pasty and white and splattered (because they have fallen from a height)

SMALL

Small-scale signs include compressions in the ground left by the animal that can be spotted using a technique called "sideheading." Facing the sun, place your ear to the ground and use your bottom eye to spot dull or shiny patches on the ground.

TRACKS

Footprints differ for each animal, but there are four basic walking patterns:

- Diagonal (e.g., dog, cat, deer): move diagonally opposite feet simultaneously

- Bounders (e.g., weasel): move front feet together and then back feet together

- Pacers (e.g., badger, skunk, porcupine, bear): move feet on one side of the body then the other

- Gallopers (e.g., rabbit, hare, rodent): push off with the back feet and land on the front feet.

The size of the track and the length of the stride tells you about the size of the animal. You can determine the weight of an animal by observing how much earth is displaced around its track.

Start fire with ice

The next time you get caught in the tundra without a box of matches, make a convex lens by polishing a piece of clear ice, which you can then use to focus sunlight to ignite your fire, like a magnifying glass.

1. Find a frozen body of water and cut out a piece of clear ice at least 3¼ in (8 cm) thick and the size of a dinner plate. Only use transparent ice.

2. Find the clearest spot and cut away the edges of your block until you have made it round, like a large hockey puck.

3. Now rub the ice around in your warm hands to polish and shape the lens, flat on one side and convex on the other.

4. You should end up with a lens that is about 5 in (12 cm) in diameter and 2½ in (6 cm) thick.

5. Position the ice lens on a stable surface so that the sunlight passes through it at right angles. Vary the height until you can see a focused spot of yellow light on the ground. Don't hold it directly above the ground because your hands will melt the ice and the drips will fall onto your tinder.

6. Place tinder (material that ignites easily—dry leaves, moss, bark, milkweed fluff, grasses, etc.) on the ground at the point where the sunlight has been focused by your ice lens. Wait for it to burst into flames.

FORECAST
the weather

You don't need satellites and powerful climate-mapping software to predict the weather. Our ancestors were very skilled at weather forecasting; they had to be because their lives and livelihood depended on it. Many sayings that today we pejoratively refer to as "old wives' tales" are actually based on sound observation of nature.

1. One cause of a red sky is dust particles in the air that scatter light at the blue end of the visible spectrum so that light at the red end of the spectrum is mainly what reaches us. "Red sky at night, sailor's delight" means that a high-pressure system is moving in from the west, which usually brings dry and pleasant weather; "red sky in the morning, sailor's warning" indicates that the high pressure and good weather has already passed and continues to head east, to make way for a low front with wet and windy weather.

2. Clouds and their direction of travel can tell you a lot about the weather. In general, white fluffy clouds indicate good weather, while dark and low clouds bring rain. "Mares' tails and mackerel scales make tall ships take in their sails" refers to cirrocumulus clouds—long streamers high in the sky, which indicate that bad weather is coming within 36 hours.

3. Increased moisture in the air (and the onset of bad weather) can be observed in household items: salt getting sticky, hair curling up at the end, knots getting tighter, spiders coming down from their webs. And if you suffer from corns, bunions, or rheumatism, your symptoms may get worse.

4. "If a circle forms round the moon, 'twill rain or snow soon" is what meteorologists refer to as a halo effect. This is an optical illusion caused by light rays from the moon being bent (diffracted) by ice crystals high up in the atmosphere (about 20,000 ft [6,100 m] above the ground in the form of thin, wispy clouds). This means than rain or snow is on the way.

5. Wind direction is a good indicator of weather. Throw a piece of grass in the air and see which direction it travels. If the grass travels west, it is being blown by an easterly wind (blowing from the east), indicating an approaching storm front; if the grass travels to the east, it is being blown by a westerly wind (blowing from the west), which means good weather.

Boil water in a cabbage leaf

If you have fire and water but no cooking vessel, you can use a cabbage leaf.

The water boils at 212°F (100°C), which is lower than the combustion point of the cabbage leaf, so while it will become charred and damaged, it won't burst into flames, partly because it also contains a lot of moisture that provides some protection.

1. Remove one of the large, thick leaves from the outside of the cabbage.

2. Make a cup-shaped depression in the coals of your fire so the cabbage leaf can sit on it and gain support from them.

3. Fill the cabbage container with water and place it in the depression.

4. When the water has boiled, carefully lift up the leaf, using at least four points of contact.

5. If the leaf is disintegrating, pour the water into another leaf that has not been exposed to the flames.

6. Another way to support the leaf is to build a triangular frame by tying three sticks together. Press the leaf into the triangular frame, fill it with water and place the frame over (but not in contact with) the coals.

Antlers are extensions of *Make an antler fishing hook* a deer's skull, and they are made out of bone tissue. Antler is a strong and versatile material, ideal for drilling and carving, and it retains its sharpness when fashioned into a fishing hook.

When working with antler, always soak the material in warm water before you begin and in between work sessions, so that it remains flexible and easier to work.

1. Choose a rounded piece of antler so that you can use the curve as part of the sides of your hook.

2. Use a pencil to draw the outline of your hook shape on the side of the antler.

3. Drill a hole where the bottom of the inside of the hook will be. Then drill a series of holes up from this first hole to create the depth of hook.

4. Run some holes out to the side of the hook to create a rough barb. Then scrape away the insides of the hook and barb until it is how you want it, before scoring and carving away the outside of the hook and shaping and reducing its thickness.

5. Scrape and smooth around the edges so that the entire hook is tubular.

6. Dry the hook then sharpen and carve a bigger recess underneath the barb if necessary.

Steam bend wood

If you enjoy working with wood, steam bending opens up a whole new repertoire of beautiful and interesting shapes.

It's simple to do and doesn't require any expensive equipment—just a boiler and a steam box.

HOW IT WORKS

When you bend wood, the outside surface stretches and the inside of the bend compresses. The steaming loosens and elasticizes the lignin— the complex polymer binding the cells, fibers, and vessels of the wood—so the fibers can easily slide past each other and compress into each other, so you can bend the wood without breaking it. The best woods for bending are hardwoods, especially white oak, hackberry, and red oak.

The wood must be straight grained, free from defects and knots, and with the grain running perfectly vertical along the face and through the length (i.e., no grain runouts, where the grain runs off the edge of the wood).

MAKE A STEAM BOX

- You can make your own steam box from four pieces of exterior plywood, 6 in (15 cm) wide, ¾ in (2cm) thick, and 3 ft 3 in (100 cm) long, and two rectangles for the ends, 6¾ in (17 cm) by 6 in (15 cm).

- Attach a series of dowels on the inside surface of the sides so you can keep the wood off the floor of the steam box, allowing the steam to circulate evenly around the wood.

- Assemble with nails and seal with polyurethane glue. Drill a couple of drainage holes in one end.

- Make two holes in the bottom and attach two dishwasher supply hoses that can then be run through the lid of a metal casserole dish, which is filled with water and heated on a stove to supply your steam for the box.

STEAM BEND YOUR WOOD

- Fire up your steamer and when the temperature has reached 200°F (93°C), carefully open one end and place your wood in the box (wear heat-resistant gloves).

- Leave the wood in the steamer for one hour per inch of thickness. So wood ¼ in (5mm) thick would need 15 minutes.

- After the time is up, carefully retrieve your wood and bend it firmly and steadily around a prepared wooden mold called a "form," and then clamp it into place.

- The wood should stay on the form for 3 to 7 days depending on the thickness and humidity.

Open a coconut with a stone

The coconut is the seed, or the fruit, of the coconut palm (*Cocos nucifera*) and botanically it isn't a nut, it's a drupe (a fruit in which an outer fleshy part surrounds a pit stone).

1. First push a pointed stick/screwdriver/skewer into the three holes in the top of the coconut (which resemble two eyes and a mouth) and drain out the juice.

2. Find a large, round, flat stone about the size of your hand and about 1½ in (4 cm) thick.

3. A line runs along the coconut from in between the two "eye" holes to the other end.

4. Hold the coconut in your hand so that this line runs from thumb to fingers (i.e., parallel to your chest).

5. Hit the edge of the stone sharply in the middle of this line and the coconut should split around its circumference, at right angles to the line.

6. To separate the flesh from the shell, hold half the coconut in your hand and insert the tip of a kitchen knife into the flesh with the sharp edge facing away from you and your wrist facing the ceiling. Cut from center to edge and pry away the flesh, then rotate a little and make another cut and so on until you have eight or nine segments of flesh.

Make a bone flute

Humans have been making and playing bone flutes for thousands of years. They are one of the most common musical instruments found in the archaeological record from Viking and Anglo Saxon times.

The oldest surviving bone flute was discovered in 2008 by archaeologists at Hohle Fels Cave in the Ach Valley, 12 mi (20 km) west of Ulm in Germany. It had been carved from the radius (wing) of a griffon vulture more than 35,000 years ago. You can make your own with more commonly available bones such as the leg bone of a lamb.

1. The interior of your bone should be hollow, but you will still have to remove the bone marrow attached to the inside. You can either use a cylindrical metal file, or you can glue coarse grit sandpaper to a stick and twist it back and forth inside the bone until the surface is smooth.

2. Make three holes in the thinner part of the bone, starting 1 in (2.5 cm) from the thin end, and about ¾ in (2 cm) apart.

3. Cut a small square hole about 1¼ in (3 cm) from the wider end, in line with the other three holes.

4. To play the flute, blow through the wide end and use three fingers of one hand to block and open the three holes.

BUILD A DRY STONE WALL

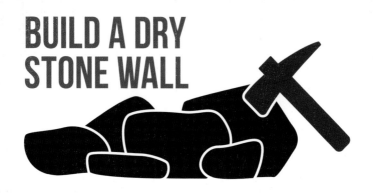

Armed only with a sharp-edged hammer and a large supply of stones, a master craftsperson can build a dry stone wall that will last for centuries.

It's like figuring out a three-dimensional jigsaw puzzle of two separate but interlocking walls. It requires the ability to look at a stone and know where it will go and (as a last resort) how to dress a stone to make it fit.

1. Always use good-quality stone, as cheaper products will be harder to work with.

2. Multiply the height by the width by the length and divide by fifteen to calculate the weight in tons of stone required. A 5 ft (1.5 m)-high dry stone wall costs about $400 for every 3 ft (1 m), and an experienced dry stone waller can build about 10 ft (3 m) in a day.

3. You will also need aggregate for the foundation and to fill in the middle of the wall.

4. First mark out a baseline and erect two wooden A-frames at each end, corresponding to the shape of the finished wall, wider at the bottom than the top. Stretch string between them to mark out the outline of the wall.

5. Dig a shallow trench along the footprint of the wall, 8 in (20 cm) deep and half as wide again as the wall and fill it with big heavy base stones and aggregate.

6. Begin building at one end (known as the quoin or cheekend) and make sure it is perfectly solid. Use a plumb line to ensure it is upright and square.

7. Build each layer (course) of the wall from either side until they meet in the middle, each new stone covering the joint between the two beneath it, like a brick wall. Pin the stones with smaller stones beneath them so that they lie securely, each stone sloping slightly downward from the center, so the rainwater runs away.

8. Fill the middle of the wall with aggregate and canter each layer in toward the center to provide stability.

9. Every 3 ft (1 m), add in a tie stone, a longer stone that spans the width of the entire wall and ties the two side walls together.

10. Lay large, flat stones along the top of the wall and then flat upright coping stones on top of them. Hammer aggregate between the coping stones to make everything solid.

TAN AN ANIMAL HIDE TO MAKE LEATHER

Tanning is the process of treating animal skin to chemically alter the protein structure so that it stops decomposing and becomes a durable leather. Untreated hide quickly rots and becomes unusable. The word "tanning" derives from the Latin *tannum*—oak bark—which is one of the ingredients that is still used in some tanning methods.

Before tanning can take place, the hide must be cured in salt and then undergo several procedures collectively known as "beamhouse operations." Here is the procedure for preparing and tanning a deer hide.

1. Staple the pelt, fur side down, to a board and then scrape away as much flesh as you can using a fleshing tool, being careful not to cut or puncture the surface.

2. Curing: Rub 3 lb (1.4 kg) of non-iodized (sea) salt on to it. Rub it into every fold and crevice so that no part of the skin escapes salting. Then leave the pelt. Remove saturated patches of salt every few hours and replace with fresh salt, until eventually all the salt becomes completely dry and crispy. This process draws moisture out of the pelt, kills bacteria, and prevents decomposition. It could take a few days or a couple of weeks, depending on the condition of the pelt.

3. Soaking: Place the pelt into a 5-gallon (23-liter) plastic trash can (NOT metal, which will react with the salt and tanning chemicals) and fill with cool, clean water. This rehydrates and softens the pelt, rinses away the salt, and helps it to absorb the tanning chemicals. Peel or scrape away the layer of dried inner skin from the hide.

4. To make the tanning solution you will need water, 1 lb (450 g) of bran flakes, 2 lb (900 g) of sea salt, 8 fl oz (225 ml) of battery acid (sulphuric acid) from a car parts store, and a box of baking soda.

5. Add the bran flakes to six pints of boiling water and leave them to soak for an hour, then drain and keep the brown water.

6. Place the sea salt into a clean 5-gallon (23-liter) plastic trash can, add one gallon of boiling water, and stir with a wooden stirrer until the salt has dissolved. Then stir in the brown bran water.

7. When the solution is lukewarm, carefully pour in the battery acid (wearing gloves and eye goggles) and stir.

8. Add the pelt and press it into the solution with the wooden stick so that every part of the pelt is soaked. Leave for forty minutes.

9. Remove the pelt and rinse it for five minutes in another 5-gallon (23-liter) plastic trash can filled with clean, lukewarm water.

10. If the leather is going to be used for clothing or furniture, add the baking soda at this point to neutralize the battery acid. If the pelt won't come into contact with human skin (e.g., it's a rug or wall hanging), this step can be skipped.

11. Remove the pelt and hang it over a board to drain and then rub a little neat's-foot oil into the damp skin.

12. Stretch the skin out and tack it onto a drying board (such as an old wooden pallet) and leave it to dry.

13. After several days when the skin feels dry but soft, lay it fur side down on a flat surface and rub the skin with a wire bristle brush to give a suede-like texture. Then set aside for a few more days until it is completely dry.

MAKE PINE PITCH

Pine pitch is made by mixing heated pine resin deposits with animal dung or some other 'filler' material to create an abundant, versatile, and sustainable substance that can be used to waterproof surfaces (such as a coracle—see page 74).

1. You can tap a pine tree to take its sap, but in any pine forest you should be able to gather plenty of natural resin deposits that have oozed from limb fractures or other breaks.

2. Punch 20 little holes in the underside of an empty soup can. Fill it with pine resin and place in a wide metal saucepan.

3. Heat the saucepan outside on a camp fire or portable stove (don't do it indoors, because the resin might ignite).

4. As the resin melts, it will run through the holes in the soup can and flow into the saucepan. Stir and press the contents of the soup can with a stick until all the resin has melted away from the impurities.

5. Remove the soup can and add two tablespoons of "filler"—dried animal dung, hair, sawdust, bone dust, etc., to the now filtered resin and stir the mixture.

6. You can either use the pine pitch now or roll bulbs of it onto sharpened sticks, allow it to cool, and then light the end to melt a controlled quantity of pitch when you need it.

Catch, skin, and cook a rabbit

Humans have been trapping and eating rabbits for thousands of years. make sure that the animal is free from disease, and cook it thoroughly to eliminate the risk of parasite infection.

CATCH YOUR RABBIT

1. Find a rabbit run—a route that you know that rabbits pass through. Look for droppings or tracks (see page 80) or remember where you have seen footprints in the snow.

2. Cut a forked branch to help direct the rabbit into your snare. Strip away the foliage then place the branch upside down in the ground so that it forms a little archway with branches on either side to funnel the rabbit through it.

3. Push extra sticks into the ground on either side of the archway and make a vertical cross with two sticks at the foot of the archway, so the rabbit has to jump to get past and gets trapped in your wire loop.

4. Using thin copper wire, make a tiny loop on one end and then feed the other end through the loop to make a noose.

5. Hang the noose so that it fills the archway above the vertical stick cross so it's about 4-6 in (10-15 cm) off the ground.

6. If a rabbit comes past, the branches will funnel it through the archway and into your wire noose.

SKIN YOUR RABBIT

1. This is best done in the field while the rabbit is fresh. Lay the rabbit on its back and make an incision through the fur on the middle of its belly from back legs to front legs.

2. Peel back the fur to reveal the belly. Cut along the belly through the skin and remove the entrails.

3. Place the rabbit on its front and make a cut in the fur in the middle of the back. Then you can strip the fur off in two pieces—over the head and over the back legs.

4. Cut through the knee joints so you are left with the drumsticks. Cut through the neck to remove the head.

5. Lay the rabbit on its back and cut either side of the pelvic bone to remove the remaining entrails; cut through and remove the tail. Rinse in cold water and soak in brine overnight.

COOK YOUR RABBIT

1. Chop two onions and crush five cloves of garlic and place them in the chest cavity. Then sew together the flaps of skin on either side of the chest.

2. Spit roast, barbecue, or cover with aluminum foil and place in a pit oven (see page 54) for two hours.

Make and throw a lasso

If you'd like to try a bit of Wild West rope action, here's the best way to make a simple lasso and use it to rustle up some frontier spirit.

MAKE YOUR LASSO

1. Take 26 ft (8 m) of thin, tough, slightly stiff rope and make a tight overhand knot at one end (make a loop and pass one end through and pull tight) for a stopper.

2. Now make a second loose overhand knot. Holding the knot in your left hand with the loop facing to the right, grab the end with your right hand and bring it around the loop and back up through the bottom of the loop and pass the end to your left hand.

3. Now you've got a second loop to the right of the first. Grab this with your right hand and pull with your left hand so the loop becomes fixed. This is called a Honda knot.

4. Reach through the Honda knot loop with the fingers of your right hand and pull some of the rope through to create a large, loose loop. That's your lasso.

TWIRL AND THROW YOUR LASSO

1. Loosen the rope through the Honda knot so you have a nice wide lasso about 2 ft (60 cm) in diameter.

2. Make another loop the same size with some of your rope slack (like coiling a hose) to form a double loop (called a "shank") and hold the shank in your right hand.

3. Begin to circle the shank above your head, keeping it horizontal.

4. Build up enough momentum so the shank stays above your head and then let go when you feel the momentum swing forward. Hold onto the other end of the rope with your left hand.

5. If your shank hits its target, pull on the rope to tighten the lasso.

Load and FIRE
a musket

A musket is a muzzle-loaded, smoothbore (no rifling in the barrel) gun that fired lead balls and was the standard infantry weapon between the 15th and 18th centuries before it was replaced by the rifle. A well-drilled infantryman could load and fire his musket up to four times a minute.

1. When you hear the command "Recover arms," bring the musket upright in front of your left shoulder and quickly check that the lock is secure and clean.

2. Place the butt on the ground between your feet and hold the barrel with your left hand at an arm's length from your body.

3. Take a cartridge from your cartridge box—a paper cylinder containing gunpowder and lead ball.

4. Tear the end off with your teeth. Pour the powder into the end of the barrel and then tip in the ball.

5. Draw the ramrod, insert it into the muzzle, and press the powder and ball firmly to the bottom of the barrel, then lift the ramrod a little and flick it down the barrel to compact the powder and ball.

6. Replace the ramrod in the pipe, raise your musket to eye level, and half cock it using your thumb.

7. Take a copper percussion cap from your cap pouch and place it on the cone at the breech end of the gun (the cap contains fulminate of mercury, which explodes to ignite the gunpowder).

8. Cock the weapon fully, place the butt firmly against your shoulder, take aim, and fire.

Make animal glue

Animal glue is made by boiling bones, hides, skin, and sinews to remove the collagen, the main structural protein of these body parts. Making glue from bones requires more processing and procedures than using hide, so here is an easy hide glue recipe.

1. Cut up scraps of animal hide or skin with a pair of scissors into small pieces, the smaller the better, preferably the size of large rolled oats.

2. Place them into an old saucepan (not one of your best pans) and cover completely with cold water.

3. Bring to a slow boil then turn down the heat and let it simmer for several hours until the hide is translucent.

4. Sieve the broth to remove the hide pieces, then return the liquid to the pan and simmer to remove more water until the liquid begins to thicken. When it has cooled enough to touch, test a little bit with your fingers to see if it's sticky. If not, return to the heat to simmer away more water.

5. Strain the liquid through a pair of tights or several layers of cheesecloth, then let it cool and set to a rubbery consistency.

6. Use a knife to chop the rubbery mass into tiny pieces and spread them out to dry.

7. Place the dry pieces into an airtight container until you want to use them (heat a few scoops with a little water but don't boil).

MAKE A CAVE PAINTING

Early Homo sapiens decorated the walls of caves with elaborate and beautiful paintings; the oldest were found in the Cave of El Castillo in northern Spain and were painted over 40,000 years ago.

1. Use charcoal or a charred stick to draw an outline of your picture on the wall.

2. Early humans used so-called "earth pigments," ground minerals mixed with spit or animal fat. You can use acrylic paints, but limit your color palette to red and yellow ocher, blood, hematite (red-brown iron oxide), manganese oxide (brown), charcoal (black), and ground calcite (lime white).

3. Like our ancestors did, mix a little animal glue (see page 104) with the pigment so that when the paint dries it will be more resistant to the moisture in the cave and last longer.

4. Apply the pigment to the wall using horsehair brushes or smearing and spraying techniques. For larger areas, smear the paint with your hands or use lichen or moss. Blow paint through a hollow animal bone for a spatter effect, or to paint around a stencil such as the splayed fingers of your hand.

5. Choose a common theme such as large wild animals—bison, horses, and deer. Human figures are rare, so avoid these.

6. Add some abstract patterns called flutings by holding three or four pigment sticks together and drawing wavy lines or scrape into the rock with parallel implements.

BLOW GLASS

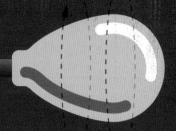

Glass blowing has been practiced since the 1st century BC, when molten glass was shaped using clay blowpipes. Today steel pipes are used, along with a steel cooling and shaping table called a marver.

One of the most famous examples of ancient glass blowing is the Portland Vase, an exquisite piece of violet-blue Roman cameo glass that is dated between AD 1 and AD 25 and is kept today in the British Museum in London.

1. Heat your supply of molten glass in the furnace to 2,125°F (1,163°C).

2. Take a steel rod and rotate the end inside the furnace to gather glass. Keep rotating evenly until you have collected a ball of glass the size of a large apple.

3. Remove the glass from the furnace, continuing to rotate so the glass doesn't drip onto the floor, and then roll it on a steel table (called a marver) to shape it into a symmetrical cylinder.

4. Blow into the pipe, then cover the end. The trapped air inside the pipe will expand to blow the glass into a bubble, called a parison.

5. Gather more glass from the furnace if required, and then marver as before. Add pigments between gatherings to create a layered color effect.

6. When you have gathered enough glass, shape it into a torpedo shape using wet newspaper then reheat in the furnace.

7. Shape the piece by rolling it on the marver while blowing into the pipe. Marver just the sides to make the bubble move down the glass; to expand the sides only marver the bottom.

8. Cut in by making score lines in the neck with large tongs called jacks. The neck should be equal to or less than the diameter of your blow-pipe. Keep rotating the pipe.

9. Transfer the piece to another rod called a punty to open the neck then reheat in the furnace and trim the lip with shears.

10. Stick your thumb over the end of the pipe and then cool the piece by dipping it into a bucket of water.

11. Place the piece on the marver and then smartly tap with a wooden block on the place where the glass joins onto the pipe and it should snap cleanly off.

12. Place the piece into an annealer (a special cooling oven that allows the glass to cool at a carefully controlled rate over the next eight hours).

Throw a pottery jug

Throwing a pot should be on everybody's bucket list. Like riding a bike, it looks easy until you try for the first time, but after a little practice to master the techniques you will wonder how you ever struggled.

Just remember to keep your hands wet and don't be afraid to show the clay who is the boss. If you go wrong, just start again.

1. Use a round lump of clay the size of a grapefruit.

2. Start the wheel rotating (control the speed with a foot pedal). Briskly throw the clay onto the center of the wheel.

3. Wet your hands and cover the clay with both hands. Press until the lump becomes uniform, then keep pressing in as you bring your hands up, to make the clay rise upward into a cylinder about 4 in (10 cm) tall. Keep wetting your hands.

4. Keeping your fingers on the outside, press down into the top of the cylinder and outward to hollow and widen the clay into a bowl.

5. Now pinch the clay between fingers and thumbs to narrow and raise the hollow cylinder.

6. Work with one hand inside the cylinder and the other on the outside. Start at the bottom of the cylinder and with the clay trapped between your hands, bring both hands upward to raise the cylinder to about 8 in (20 cm) while narrowing the sides.

7. Place your hand inside and gently press outward to make the middle bulbous, keeping the top and bottom the same width as before.

8. Place your hands around the outside of the rim (as if you were choking it) and gently squeeze to narrow the rim.

9. Trap the rim between your fingers and thumb and move outward so that the lip curls.

10. Smooth the inside with a piece of sponge on a stick.

11. Stop the wheel and make the spout by pressing down on the rim with your index finger while supporting the edges of the spout with the fingers of your other hand.

12. When the jug has dried until it's as hard as soft leather, roll another piece of clay into a narrow cylinder. Fix one end to the edge of a table and stroke downward with wet fingers to stretch the clay until you have about 12 in (30 cm)—enough to make the handle.

13. Score the two places where the handle will join to the jug (opposite the spout) and then apply slip (thick watery clay) to the scored area.

14. Attach the top of the handle first by pressing it into the slip, then smudge the edge so that it is pressed into the pot.

15. Curl the handle over and attach the bottom of the handle to the slip. Nip off any excess and then smudge the edge where it meets the pot, making sure that the handle is straight and perpendicular to the pot surface.

Knot two ropes together

One of the best ways to join two ropes together is the "double fisherman."

All ropes have a tensile strength, which is the load at which they can be expected to break. The rope's working load is calculated by dividing the tensile strength by a factor to give a comfortable safety margin. Adding a knot between two ropes inevitably lowers the working load by as much as 50 percent. The double fisherman is said to decrease the working load by between 25 and 40 percent.

1. Place the two ends of the ropes parallel to each other.

2. Loop the end of one rope around the other twice, so the second loop goes over the first rope and then back up the other side.

3. Feed the end back through the two loops and pull tight.

4. Repeat steps 2 and 3 using the other rope in the opposite direction.

5. Slide the two knots together by pulling the standing lines.

Cross a desert

You have four options: traveling on foot, by vehicle, by camel, or dragging a cart. If you are inexperienced, your best options are probably foot and vehicle.

1. Leave a copy of your itinerary, route map, and travel times with someone you trust. If you don't return within an agreed time, they can raise the alarm.

2. The most important consideration is to carry enough water and replace minerals lost through sweat. Carry a minimum of 7 pints (4 liters) of water per person per day. Drink frequently and don't wait until you are thirsty. Drink enough water to keep your urine clear. Individual requirements differ but if you are a novice, pack too much rather than too little. Look out for signs of dehydration. If you have a headache, dry eyes, nosebleeds, sore throat and lungs, or muscle cramps, you are already badly dehydrated. Rehydrate and rest.

3. Pack energy-rich, high-protein food with lots of calories and good carbohydrates for energy. Consume electrolyte snacks to replace sodium, potassium, magnesium, and calcium.

4. Minimize water loss by moving slowly, travelling at night (when the moon is full) when it is cool, and sleeping during the day. Protect against heat exhaustion and heat stroke by wearing lightweight, light-colored, long-sleeve cotton clothing and a wide-brimmed hat to reflect the heat. Wear sunglasses to protect your eyes, otherwise you can get sand blindness from the glare.

5. Avoid spiders, scorpions, and snakes by never leaving your backpack unattended and sleeping away from rocks and bushes. Avoid walking barefoot.

6. If travelling by car, carry extra water for your car's radiator and make sure your car is in good working order. Make sure you can mend a tire and know some basic maintenance. Fill up with gas whenever you get the chance. If your car breaks down, stay with it. Try to find some shade near the car or rest in the shade of the car.

7. If you encounter a sandstorm, put a piece of moistened cloth over your nose and mouth, and protect your eyes. Head for high ground, where the storm will be less forceful. If you have a camel, make it sit down and press yourself against its leeward side. If you are among sand dunes, do not seek shelter right on the leeward side of the dune or you could become buried. If you are in a vehicle, you may be able to outdrive the storm. If not, drive the car off the road so that when visibility reduces you won't risk a collision. Close the windows and the vents.

Treat a snake bite

While most snake bites aren't fatal and many snakes aren't dangerous to humans, the safest reaction to a snake bite is to act on the assumption that it is poisonous and seek immediate medical attention.

While you are waiting for professional help, follow these steps to reduce your risk of serious harm.

1. Carefully move away from the snake so you can't be bitten a second time.

2. Make a note of the snake's appearance and if possible, take a photograph. This will enable the doctor to identify the snake and give you the appropriate antivenom.

3. Don't run or do anything to increase your heart rate as this will spread the venom around your body more quickly.

4. When you are a safe distance away from the snake, lie down, keep as still as possible, and take slow, deep breaths.

5. Remove clothing, jewelry, and other constricting items from the bite area, which may start to swell. If possible, cover the bite with a sterile bandage.

6. Do not attempt to suck out the poison. Do not cut away tissue, or apply a tourniquet or ice.

7. If you can't get medical attention, lie still for several hours and wait for the venom to leave your body.

CATCH AN EEL

Eels are elongated fish, ranging in length from 2 in (5 cm) to 13 ft (4 m). An adult eel can weigh over 55 lb (25 kg). The best time and place to catch them is on a summer's night in fresh water when the eels are migrating to the sea to breed.

1. Look for underwater features such as gravel bars, plateaus, shallows, tree roots, and sunken bushes that make good ambush points. Eels are territorial, so just because someone caught some eels a few nights ago doesn't mean you will have luck in the same place, because the territory may now be temporarily fished out (empty).

2. Use a fyke—a long, conical net supported by hoops with three internal funnels, with successively smaller entrances. Place your net underwater with the entrances facing upstream and a few hours before dusk, bait with a mixture of chopped worms, old fish, maggots, or even chicken liver.

3. You can also catch an eel with a rod, but you don't always have to use a hook. Make a bob by wrapping a strip of mackerel with wool. When the eel bites the bob, the wool gets caught up in its numerous hook-like teeth, allowing you to reel it in. Eels have an exceptional sense of smell, so chum the water with fish guts before casting your line.

Collect sap and make maple syrup

Maple trees are ready for tapping in early spring when the temperatures have warmed up above freezing and the trees have started to draw sap. The sap comes up from the roots, which store starch over the winter until it gets converted into sugars.

During the spring, capillary action draws the sap up the tree to provide the nutrients to grow new shoots and leaves. The clear sap is called sweet water; it is 98 percent water.

The sugar or rock maple (*Acer saccharum*) and the black maple (*Acer nigrum*) give the best syrup, but some people also tap the red maple.

1. Find a large, old sugar maple with a diameter of at least 20 in (50 cm).

2. Drill a hole into the tree at a slight upward angle using a ⅜ in drill bit. Go into the tree about 1½ in (4 cm). A big maple tree can

have two or three taps (metal spouts) on it, at different sides of the trunk, without doing any harm. The most productive tap will be on the side that receives the most sun.

3. Insert the tap into the hole and gently drive it into place with a hammer so that it is tight. The sap should start dripping out immediately.

4. Cut a slit near the top of a large plastic milk container and slide it onto the tap. Leave the lid on. Alternatively, you could leave your container on the ground and run a plastic tube into it from the tap.

5. Each tap will supply about 80 pints (45 liters) over a four-week period and it takes 70 pints (40 liters) of sap to make 1¾ pints (1 liter) of syrup. Each tree produces thousands of pints of sap, so what you tap won't harm the tree.

6. Store the sap below 38°F (3°C) until you are ready to boil it down to concentrate the sugars to make maple syrup.

7. Boil down the sap for several hours in a large, flat pan (the bigger the surface area the better, but a large metal stockpot is acceptable). Keep scooping away the white deposit that forms on the surface of the liquid. The sap will become darker as you boil off the water.

8. Use a thermometer to test the boiling point. When the remaining dark liquid begins to boil at 7.5°F (4°C) above the local boiling point of water, you officially have maple syrup. While warm, pour it into sterile jars and seal.

SHARPEN
a knife

One of the most important rules of the culinary arts is always to work with a sharp knife. Using a blunt knife is not just inconvenient, it's actually dangerous. You have to use more effort with a blunt knife, which increases the chance of the blade slipping and causing injury.

USING A WHETSTONE

1. Choose the correct angle to sharpen your knife, preferably the angle used by the manufacturer (check on the packaging when you purchase a new knife). A shallow angle (10 degrees) makes a sharper but less durable edge; a steeper angle (30 degrees) is more durable.

2. If you don't know the correct angle for your knife, choose a compromise of 22 degrees. You can judge this by holding the knife at right angles to the stone, then tilt to 45 degrees and then roughly halve the angle again to get 22 degrees.

3. Apply the appropriate lubrication to your whetstone: water, oil, or nothing. Some stones are ruined by oil so check with the manufacturer.

4. Place the whetstone on a flat surface lengthways in front of you and hold the knife in your right hand with the blade facing away from you. Keep your left hand on the blade, helping to guide and maintain the angle. Pass the blade left to right over the stone as if you were trying to cut a very thin slice off it (make sure you run along the entire blade with each stroke from heel to tip). After ten strokes, turn the knife over so that your left hand is holding the handle and your right hand is on the blade, guiding. Make ten strokes from right to left.

5. Start with the coarse side of the whetstone to grind the edge and remove a lot of metal, then finish off with the fine grit side to sharpen (hone) the knife.

USING A HONING STEEL

1. A safe beginner's method is to place a tea towel on the work surface and hold the steel vertically with the tip resting on the towel. Then run the knife down the right edge of the steel, starting at the heel and ending at the tip. After ten strokes, keeping the handle in your same hand, run the blade ten times down the left side of the steel.

2. After sharpening, rinse and dry the blade to remove any grit and metal filings before you start cutting food.

Start a FIRE in the rain

Starting a fire in wet conditions depends on knowing where to find dry tinder (or being prepared and carrying some dry tinder in your backpack). Sometimes lighting a fire makes the difference between comfort and hypothermia, so these tips could one day save your life.

1. You can harvest lots of tinder underneath a fallen tree, such as dried leaves, grass, and sawdust. Scrape away at the underside of the rotting wood for more dry sawdust and look out for fungus growing under the tree, which can also be added to your tinder hoard.

2. You can also harvest standing deadwood where you can break into the trunk and find "fat lighter," which you can use as kindling or break into small shavings for tinder. Fat lighter is the heartwood of pine trees. It is saturated in crystallized resin and can usually be found in pine tree stumps or in the joints where limbs intersect the trunk.

3. Look for scar tissue on a damaged pine tree (e.g., from a lightning strike) where the bark has scarred over with resin. Harvest these clumps of wood and resin for a flammable fire starter. Wait until the fatwood has completely burned away before cooking on the fire, otherwise its oily, sooty smoke will spoil the food.

4. Birch bark is ideal tinder. You can harvest it from a live tree by peeling away some of the wet layers until you reach the crisp white and dry bark, which looks like shreds of wallpaper. Crumble it up into smaller pieces for tinder.

5. You can supplement your kindling by making fuzz sticks. Find a branch about 1½ in (4 cm) thick and strip away the wet bark with a sharp knife. Then pare thin slices until you reach dry wood; you can remove flakes of wood to use as tinder, or create a fuzz stick by leaving the slices joined to the branch. A fuzz stick will light much more readily than a regular branch.

6. If you plan to camp in the rain, you can pack some little fire-lighting bricks (used to light a barbecue), or a cotton ball coated in petroleum jelly (rip it open to expose the fibers before lighting).

COPPICE FOR *firewood*

Coppicing is a very old woodland management technique that produces fast-growing, sustainable timber without killing a tree.

Humans have been coppicing since Neolithic times. The decline in woodland area over the centuries has been caused in part by the decline in coppicing as the demands for charcoal and wood fuel have been replaced by "modern" fuels, along with the traditional crafts such as weaving that coppicing also sustained.

Many species of tree can be coppiced, which involves cutting the tree down to a stump (the interval between coppicing ranges from 3 to 50 years depending on the tree species). Since the coppiced trees already have a fully developed root system, they grow back quickly and stronger than before and their lifespan is considerably increased. Another advantage of coppiced wood is that because the wood is thinner it takes less time to season. It is also good for wildlife and biodiversity as it opens up the ground around the stump, letting in light and allowing new plants and nearby trees to thrive.

Sweet chestnut, hazel, and hornbeam are the most commonly coppiced tree species but many other types of deciduous tree can be coppiced: alder, ash, beech, birch, field maple, oak (which has a 50-year cycle), sycamore, and willow. However, some species fare better than others. For example, if an ash is coppiced in mid- or late winter, the stump may not grow new shoots for 15 months.

- The trees must be cut during the winter before the sap has risen.

- Cut all the branches low, leaving 4-6 in (10-15 cm) of stump above the ground.

- A typical coppiced woodland should also include plenty of regular trees that are allowed to grow normally, interspersed with coppiced trees at various stages in their cycle, for maximum biodiversity.

- You should expect to see a mass of new shoots by the end of the following year. Natural competition means that this mass will thin down as the stronger shoots outperform the weaker ones, which will die back, leaving you with fewer. This is perfectly natural, so don't panic.

- However, one thing that will hamper shoot growth is grass around the base, which will compete for water. Lay some tree matting to restrict grass growth.

- Don't be tempted to coppice conifers. With the notable exception of yew, they will not grow back.

Remove a stone from a horse's hoof

Picking out hooves should be done daily before and after riding to keep them healthy. If you neglect this important task, the horse may experience terrible discomfort and eventually go lame.

1. When your horse is tied up and calm, stroke him gently on the neck and shoulder, speaking softly. Stand near the shoulder and face the tail.

2. Run your hand down its leg and tap the back of the leg to warn it that you want it to bend the leg so you can pick it up (this gives the horse a chance to balance itself).

3. Squeeze the leg above the fetlock. If this doesn't work, gently squeeze the hard, oval growth above the knee on the inside of the leg (the chestnut). The leg should lift in line with the thigh (don't pull it sideways toward you; this will injure the knee).

4. Hold the hoof in one hand, and with the other hand, use a hoof pick and brush to remove compacted mud and stones, working from heel to toe. On the tender middle portion (the frog), just use your hand. If the frog looks raggedy, you may need to call a farrier to trim it for you.

5. Check for thrush—white flaky deposits on the hoof or frog. Check that the sole of the hoof is hard and concave and see if it needs trimming.

NAVIGATE USING STICKS AND *SHADOWS*

If you don't have a compass, you can still orient yourself as long as there is enough sunlight to cast a shadow.

The sun always rises in the east and takes between 10 and 14 hours to travel in an arc across the sky before it sets in the west.

1. Find a straight stick about 3ft 3 in (1 m) long and stick it vertically in the ground.

2. The stick casts a shadow on the ground. Place a small marker on the top of the stick's shadow.

3. Wait for at least 30 minutes (or longer to gain a more accurate measurement).

4. The shadow will move on the ground as the earth rotates. After your time is up, place a marker on the new top of the stick's shadow.

5. A line drawn between the two points will run from west to east because the shadow has moved from west to east (the opposite of the sun's movement).

6. Stand with your back to the stick, with your left foot on the first marker and your right foot on the second marker. You are now facing north and south is directly behind you.

TREAT HYPOTHERMIA

Hypothermia occurs when the body loses heat faster than it can generate it. When this happens, the core temperature drops below that required for normal metabolism.

The normal body temperature is 97.7–99.5°F (36.5–37.5°C). Hypothermia occurs when the core temperature drops below 95°F (35°C).

Symptoms include shivering (although this stops during extreme hypothermia), exhaustion, slurred speech and memory loss, drowsiness, and confusion. Infants also display bright red, cold skin. If you suspect someone has hypothermia, call emergency services and then follow these instructions:

1. Remove the victim from the conditions that caused the hypothermia: take them out of cold water or place a barrier between them and the snow, wind, or rain (use your own body if necessary).

2. Wet clothes will continue to reduce body temperature as the water evaporates, but only remove wet clothing if you can supply dry blankets or clothing in their place.

3. Warm up the center of the body (chest and groin) as well as the neck and head. Use skin to skin contact under layers of blankets. You may use an electric blanket, but nothing really hot or wet (no hot baths, heating pads, unprotected hot water bottles, or steaming towels).

4. Don't warm the arms or legs as this will be at the expense of the vital organs such as the heart, lungs, and brain. Don't massage or perform brisk rubbing.

5. If the victim is conscious, give them a hot, nonalcoholic, decaffeinated drink such as hot chocolate. Sweet snacks, high in carbohydrates, are also allowed, since they provide energy to heat the body.

READ A C🧭MPASS

Learning how to use a compass is an important outdoor skill. You should never venture into the wilderness without one, even if you are driving.

A compass can help you find your bearings and walk to safety, especially when visibility is poor, even if you have no idea where you are.

COMPASS ANATOMY

Inside every compass is a magnetic "needle" that rotates around a central pivot. The red end always points to the earth's magnetic north pole, and an outer dial is marked with the cardinal points N, E, S, and W (North, East, South, and West). The edge of the housing is numbered from 0 to 360, counting in multiples of 20, and every 2 degrees is marked with a line.

NOTICE YOUR SURROUNDINGS

Even though you are using a compass, you must still be attentive to your surroundings. Make a mental note of important features, such as a mountain or a line of trees, because you can use these to help you stay on course once you have established your direction of travel with the compass.

ORIENTEERING COMPASS

An orienteering compass includes a transparent baseplate with orienting lines; the big arrow at the end of the baseplate is called the "direction of travel arrow." If you want to travel southwest, turn the dial so that this arrow is lined up halfway between south and west. Keeping the compass flat on your palm, turn your body until the red arrow points to N on the compass housing. Now the direction of travel arrow will be pointing southwest. Locate a feature in the distance to which this arrow is pointing and walk toward it. Keep the compass around your neck and check your bearings every fifteen minutes to keep you on course.

USING A COMPASS AND MAP

North on your map and north on your compass will differ by several degrees depending on your location on the earth. This difference is called "declination" and is usually marked on a map so you can correct for it by turning the compass housing right or left the requisite number of degrees.

To follow a route on a map,, line up your starting position with your destination along the edge of the compass, with the direction of travel arrow pointing at your destination. Then carefully turn the compass housing until the orienting lines on the compass housing line up with the vertical meridian lines on the map. Then hold the compass flat in your hand and turn your body until the red arrow lines up with N on the compass housing and look at the direction of travel arrow, which will now be pointing at your destination.

Forage for food

Foraged food is a winner on all fronts—it's free, packed with nutrients, and gets you walking in the fresh air.

All you have to remember is to stay within your knowledge and comfort zone so you don't end up picking something harmful.

MUSHROOMS

Be very, very careful about what you collect. There are stories of experts requiring a kidney transplant after ingesting poisonous fungi. The simplest rule for mushroom picking is to learn how to identify a few edible species and pick only them. Also, you must learn to recognize any poisonous species with which they might be confused. Buy field guides or take a course and if you are in any doubt—don't eat it.

WILD GARLIC

Wild garlic is harvestable throughout the year. It is like cultivated garlic but milder. It grows in woodland, near or among bluebells. You can eat the bulbs, and the leaves and flowers make a great addition to salads or a garnish for cheese sandwiches. Avoid poisonous lily-of-the-valley, which looks similar but doesn't smell of garlic.

NETTLES

Packed with vitamins, minerals, and more vitamin C than oranges, nettles can be used to make tea and soup or as a substitute for baby spinach. However, you should only harvest the youngest leaves (no larger than about 2¾ in [7 cm] wide) in early spring before the flowers appear because the mature leaves can damage the kidneys.

DANDELIONS

These abundant weeds are very versatile. You can use the leaves in salads or as a sandwich garnish. The mild-tasting and faintly sweet yellow flowers are a rich source of the nutrient lecithin. They can be used in everything from omelettes and couscous to risottos or dipped in seasoned flour and fried. Grind up the roots to make coffee.

ELDERBERRY

Elderberry (or "elder") is plentiful in hedgerows, woodland, and even by the side of the road. You can eat the sweet white flowers raw or use them as an ingredient in lots of foods, from cakes and cookies to ice cream, jam, and wine. Harvest this elegant, low-growing shrub on bright, sunny mornings during the early summer. Make sure the plant is woody-stemmed, otherwise you may be picking goutweed (or "ground elder"), which isn't poisonous, but is less pleasant and a mild laxative.

Work the land with a horse and plow

The old-fashioned skill of plowing with horses is a wonderful antidote to the stress and strain of modern life. It allows you to work in the moment with skill and precision and to experience a unique bond between you, your team of horses, and the land.

1. Use quiet, well-behaved horses that obey stop and turn commands and that walk slowly and calmly even when they encounter obstacles (e.g., rocks) and surprises (e.g., a ground hornet nest).

2. Inspect the plow's handles and beam to ensure they are free from cracks.

3. Hitch your horses to the plow, step them ahead until the traces are tight, and stop them. Tie your lines in a knot, pass them over your left shoulder, against your neck and under your right arm. This stops you from being dragged along if the horses get spooked.

4. If you're a beginner, use stakes to measure out a plot to plow measuring about 50 ft by 100 ft (15 m by 30 m). Any smaller than this and you will spend too much time turning the horses around. Plow straight from one stake to another and look at the stake, not at the plow.

5. Once you start plowing, adjust the length of the lines so they are just right; too loose and the horses will go too fast; too tight and you will be pulled forward.

6. Walk slowly. Raise the handles slightly to deepen the furrow; push down to raise the plow out of the ground. Raise the right handle to steer right and the left handle to turn left. Stay calm and use gentle control.

7. Don't fight the plow. If it jumps out, stop the horses and back them up as you pull the plow backward.

8. To turn at the end of a furrow, tip the plow to the right so that it rides on the plowshare and the right handle. Turn your horses around to the right and pull the plow back (you always turn right at the end of a furrow).

9. Stop the horses when they are right next to the upturned soil of the previous furrow, then raise both handles slightly and walk them on. You walk in the furrow you are making, and your near horse walks in the furrow you are covering.

10. At the end of the day, start the next furrow and leave the plow buried in the soil to protect it from rusting.

MAKE TEA AND FLAVORED HONEY FROM PINE NEEDLES

Pine needles contain a huge dose of vitamin C (eight times the amount found in orange juice) and also provide vitamin A, several B vitamins, and antioxidants.

However, not all species of pine are safe to use, while other plants might look like pine but should be avoided. The most commonly used pine for consumption is white pine, which is easily recognized by its long, soft needles.

1. The younger, bright green, shorter, and softer needles are the most suitable; they have more flavor and nutrients than older needles, which can also be more bitter.

2. Use a sharp knife to remove the needles from the central twig.

3. Rinse, crush, and chop the needles into small sections to help release the oils and nutrients when the needles are boiled.

PINE TEA

This is a traditional decongestant that will perk you up and improve mental clarity.

1. For a mild cup, pour boiling water into a mug, then add some chopped needles and leave them to brew for 5–10 minutes. They will sink to the bottom of the mug, so you don't have to remove them before you drink.

2. For a strong and more medicinal brew, boil the leaves in a saucepan of water for 3 minutes, then remove from the heat and leave to steep for 5–10 minutes before pouring into a mug. Add sugar and/or cinnamon to your taste.

PINE HONEY

You can make your own honey from scratch or infuse store-bought honey with your needles.

INFUSION

1. Oven dry the pine needles by baking them on a tray lined with baking paper at 150°F (70°C) with the oven door slightly open.

2. Crumble the dried needles into the bottom of a sterile jar and fill up with honey. Stir well and screw on the lid. Let the herbs infuse for one week, then strain into another sterile jar.

MAKE YOUR OWN

1. Boil 2.2 lb (1 kg) fresh pine needles in 7 pints (4 liters) of water.

2. Leave covered for 2 days, then strain through a linen cloth.

3. Add 1 lb (450 g) of raw sugar and 1 jar of honey; simmer until thick.

4. Pour into sterile jars while the mixture is still warm.

Carve a WOODEN BOWL

The beauty of carving a bowl from wood is that you can make it as simple or ornate as you like, limited only by your skill and time available.

Sharpen your tools before you start, and always keep your hands and fingers behind the path of the cutting tool.

1. Choose your wood. You can carve green, dry, or seasoned wood. Green wood is the easiest but it may crack and separate as it dries, destroying your creation. In general, nut trees and hardwoods are better for carving than fruit trees.

2. Select a round log and cleave it down the middle using a splitting wedge and lump hammer through the grain so that when you carve, it will be with, rather than against, the grain.

3. Take one of the halves and use an ax to tidy up the flat, bare wood so that you reach a uniform top layer of grain.

4. Remove the bark using a draw knife (a blade with a handle at each end). Work from the center of the log toward you, not the entire length at once.

5. Draw a rough outline of the bowl shape onto the curved face of the log.

6. Place on a solid surface and roughly shape each end to a symmetrical oval with an ax. Flatten the bottom to make the bowl more stable.

7. Smooth the rough surface of the bowl block with a rasp and further refine using a selection of spokeshaves.

8. Draw an oval on the top of the bowl, leaving at least ¾ in (2 cm) around the edge of the wood.

9. Hollow out the interior first with a curved hand adze and then use a variety of gouges (curved chisels) to shape and smooth the surface. Always carve in from the lip to the bottom. Use a calliper or bowl gauge to help you reduce the walls to a uniform thickness, which will reduce cracks and warping as the wood dries.

10. Soften the sharp edge of the rim using a rasp or paring knife.

11. Don't use sandpaper to finish your hand-carved bowl; it will completely destroy the attractive hand-carved patina and leave grit embedded in the wood grain.

12. If the wood is green, store the bowl in a cool, humid place for six months to dry out. Weigh it periodically; when it stops losing weight (water), it is ready. Rub flaxseed oil onto the surface with your hands, then leave to cure for another month before use.

MAKE A BIRCH BARK CONTAINER

Birch bark is beautiful, durable, and flexible, the ideal qualities for making a simple and stylish cylindrical container.

Collect your birch bark, about 0.04 in (1 mm) thick, during the summer from naturally fallen trees. You can strip the outer bark from a living tree without killing it, so long as you don't damage the inner bark, but the first option is clearly preferable. Remove large pieces at least 30 in (75 cm) long and 8 in (20 cm) wide.

Birch bark is a good material for food containers because it contains a preservative that helps to protect food. It is a scarce resource, so take extra care to make a quality item that will last for several years.

1. Use a craft knife to cut the edges of your strip into a clean rectangle, about 20 in (50 cm) long and 6 in (15 cm) wide.

2. Remove any loose material and algae from the outside of the bark, to reveal the clean, smooth birch bark underneath.

3. Roll the bark into a cylinder so the wood doubles up tightly with no spaces between the layers. If you are going to use the container for food, make sure the smooth side of the bark is on the inside of the container so none of the surface can flake into your food.

4. Use a bradawl to punch a row of eight equally spaced holes on either side of the outside seam. Start by making the two pairs of holes at either end and then stick a nail or wooden peg through them to hold the cylinder together while you make the other holes.

5. Cross thread a lace into the holes using a leather lace, spruce roots, or other natural cordage. You might need to use a small, curved needle to thread the middle holes.

6. Tie off the lace inside the cylinder, so the outside looks neat.

7. Use a craft knife to trim the top and bottom of the cylinder so that the edges are horizontal.

8. Cut two thin disks from a branch of seasoned wood that is the same diameter as your cylinder for the lid and base. Taper the lid slightly into a stopper shape.

9. Attach the base by making holes with a bradawl, then gently hammer in hawthorns and trim off the ends so they are flush. You can also use wood glue on the circumference of the base for added security.

Prevent and treat
MOSQUITO BITES

Mosquitoes are the most dangerous creatures known to humans; they are responsible for spreading a host of serious diseases including malaria, west nile virus, yellow fever, and dengue fever. Sharks kill four people every year; mosquitoes kill one million.

1. The best way to avoid being bitten by a mosquito is to avoid places where they live, but they are found all over the world (except Antarctica) anywhere where there is fresh water for their larvae. However, they are more common in warm, wet areas, close to the equator.

2. Avoid standing water: lakes, swamps, creeks, bogs, etc., especially when it is hot.

3. Wear mosquito repellent. The most popular repellents contain between 30 and 50 percent DEET (N,N-diethyl-m-toluamide), which is reported to be safe for use from 2 months old. You can also spray your clothes (but not skin) with repellent containing permethrin.

4. If you prefer to use more natural repellents, the lemony natural plant oil citronella repels mosquitoes, black flies, fleas, and ticks. Diluted properly in a base oil, it can be sprayed on your skin and clothing, or you can buy insect-repellent citronella candles.

5. Keep your skin covered. Wear light-colored, loose, long-sleeved shirts and long pants. This provides a barrier between your skin and the mosquitoes. It also helps to keep you cool, which helps because mosquitoes are attracted to heat and sweat.

6. Try not to exert yourself because the increase in carbon dioxide from your breath will also attract mosquitoes (as well as making you hot).

7. Sleep inside a mosquito net, which stretches like a funnel over your bed and allows air to circulate but has mesh which is too fine for the mosquitoes to penetrate. Don't allow your bare flesh to make contact with the net, otherwise a mosquito could stick its mouthparts through and bite you.

8. If you get bitten, the site will itch as your body reacts to the mosquito's saliva. Wash the area with warm, soapy water and apply an ice pack to reduce the swelling. If you can't find clean water, rub with an alcohol wipe to clean and cool the area. Don't scratch, however tempting, because this will make the itching worse and increase the chance of infection. If the swelling is severe, use an antihistamine cream. If an infection develops, see a doctor immediately.

Store food without a fridge

There are four major ways to preserve food without refrigeration: curing (see page 64), appropriate storage, drying, and canning. We have become so used to stuffing the contents of our shopping bags into that magic white box in the kitchen that most of us have lost skills that would have been common knowledge in times past.

Refrigerators have their limitations, namely that we sometimes leave food for several weeks before consumption. Although the food is still edible, it can lose a considerable proportion of its taste and nutrition. Old-fashioned methods preserve taste and goodness.

SIMPLE STORAGE

Leave perishables (not meat or dairy) in a cool, dry place, such as a cellar at a temperature of between 50 and 55°F (10 and 13°C). Most root crops and some fruits can be stored in this way.

Choose firm, healthy, intact fruit and vegetables with no bruising. Brush away dirt but don't wash with water. Store the produce in slatted boxes to allow plenty of air circulation, or place them on shelves (don't stack broccoli, celery, Brussels sprouts, cauliflower, melons, or quince). Handle with care as you transport them to the cellar, as any bruising will encourage decay.

DRYING

Archaeological evidence shows that humans have been drying food for at least 6,000 years. This process deprives the microorganisms that make food rot of the moist conditions they need to survive and multiply. Dried foods can be stored indefinitely so long as they remain dry.

A wide range of food is suitable for drying, from tuberous and bulbous root vegetables, herbs and fruits to pod beans, cereal, and bread grains. Wash fruit and vegetables well before drying. Some experts also advise pasteurizing the food before drying by heating in an oven at 175°F (80°C) for 10–15 minutes.

Pulp method: Mash the food and then spread the pulp on a flat, clean surface until it is about 2½ in (6 cm) thick and leave it to dry in the sun.

Cubing method: Cut the food into cubes, thread them onto string, and hang outside in the sun to dry.

Chopping method: Cut the food into slices and lay them out on cheesecloth stretched over a wooden frame. Cover with more cheesecloth and leave in the sun, turning the slices occasionally.

In all thee methods, move the produce under shelter at night to guard from dampness and dew.

CANNING

Fruit and vegetables can be canned at home but you must follow the steps precisely and do everything at the correct time. Here is a brief overview of the canning process, but if you want to try canning, consult a specialized canning guide to learn what preparation each food requires. The basic steps are sterilizing your containers (glass or cans) by boiling them in water for ten minutes; preparing the ingredients (e.g., washing, peeling, chopping); filling the jars (foods are either "hot-packed" or "old-packed"); leaving space at the top; adding preservatives; removing air bubbles; sealing and labelling.

As long as vegetables are canned soon after picking, they retain nearly all of their vitamins and minerals.